Scripture Works!

Effectively Praying God's Word over Life Situations

...Faith without works is dead! – James 2:17

RALI MACAULAY

Unless otherwise noted, all Scripture quotations are taken from the King James Version (KJV): KING JAMES VERSION, public domain.

Scripture quotations marked (NIV) are taken from the Holy Bible, New International Version®, NIV®. Copyright © 1973, 1978, 1984, 2011 by Biblica, Inc.™ Used by permission of Zondervan. All rights reserved worldwide.

Scripture quotations marked (NLT) are taken from the Holy Bible, New Living Translation, copyright © 1996, 2004, 2007 by Tyndale House Foundation. Used by permission of Tyndale House Publishers, Inc., Carol Stream, Illinois 60188. All rights reserved.

Scripture quotations marked (AMP) are taken from the Amplified® Bible, Copyright © 1954, 1958, 1962, 1964, 1965, 1987 by The Lockman Foundation Used by permission." (www.Lockman.org)

Scripture quotations marked (GNT) are from the Good News Translation in Today's English Version- Second Edition Copyright © 1992 by American Bible Society. Used by Permission.

Scripture quotations marked (MSG) are taken from The Message. Copyright © 1993, 1994, 1995, 1996, 2000, 2001, 2002. Used by permission of NavPress Publishing Group."

Scripture quotations marked (NASB) are taken from the New American Standard Bible®, Copyright © 1960, 1962, 1963, 1968, 1971, 1972, 1973, 1975, 1977, 1995 by The Lockman Foundation. Used by permission." (www.Lockman.org)

Scripture quotations marked (NKJV) are taken from the New King James Version®. Copyright © 1982 by Thomas Nelson. Used by permission. All rights reserved.

Scripture quotations marked (ERV) are taken from the HOLY BIBLE: EASY-TO-READ VERSION © 2001 by World Bible Translation Center, Inc. and used by permission.

Scripture quotations marked (ESV)are from the ESV Bible (The Holy Bible, English Standard Version), copyright © 2001 by Crossway Bibles, a publishing ministry of Good News Publishers. Used by permission. All rights reserved.

Copyright © 2014 Rali Macaulay/Wellspring Inspirations
All rights reserved.
Get more resources online at: www.wellspringinspirations.com

ISBN-13: 978-1484801277
ISBN-10: 148480127X

All rights reserved. No part of this publication may be reproduced in any form or by any electronic or mechanical means including information storage and retrieval systems – except for brief quotations in articles or reviews – without the prior permission from the publisher.

DEDICATION

To my Lord and Savior, Jesus Christ. I am grateful for your unfailing love and faithfulness that has brought me this far; and keeps me going. Thank you for choosing me for this assignment, and for the grace for completion.

To my husband, Ibukunoluwa. In so many ways, I have learnt the unfailing love of God through you. Thank you for believing in me, and for the gentle nudges along the journey of completing this book.

To my precious little children, Ara, Ini and Eri. You make life so meaningful, and I feel so blessed to be your mother. Love you all so much!

To my mother. Thank you for teaching me the virtues of discipline, hard work, and determination.

To my siblings, family and friends. You all have enriched my life with your friendship, support and prayers; and I'm blessed to have you all in my life.

Presented To:

_____

From:

_____

Date:_____

CONTENTS

    Preface   I

    Introduction   III

1. Scripture Works for Abundance   Pg 1
2. Scripture Works for Assurance   Pg 3
3. Scripture Works for The Blessing   Pg 5
4. Scripture Works for Breakthrough   Pg 8
5. Scripture Works for Business   Pg 11
6. Scripture Works for Career and Work   Pg 15
7. Scripture Works for Children   Pg 18
8. Scripture Works for Courage   Pg 22
9. Scripture Works for Debt Freedom   Pg 24
10. Scripture Works for Deliverance   Pg 29
11. Scripture Works for Employment Interview   Pg 33
12. Scripture Works for Enlightenment/Direction/Guidance   Pg 36
13. Scripture Works for Faith   Pg 38
14. Scripture Works for Favor   Pg 41
15. Scripture Works for Financial Increase & Prosperity   Pg 43
16. Scripture Works for Forgiveness   Pg 46
17. Scripture Works for Gainful Employment   Pg 48
18. Scripture Works for Gifts & Talents   Pg 52

19	Scripture Works for Healing	Pg 55
20	Scripture Works for Help	Pg 59
21	Scripture Works for Husbands	Pg 62
22	Scripture Works for Joy	Pg 65
23	Scripture Works for Longevity	Pg 68
24	Scripture Works for Love	Pg 71
25	Scripture Works for Marriage	Pg 74
26	Scripture Works for Overcoming Condemnation	Pg 78
27	Scripture Works for Overcoming Depression	Pg 81
28	Scripture Works for Overcoming Fear	Pg 85
29	Scripture Works for Overcoming Grief & Sorrow	Pg 88
30	Scripture Works for Peace	Pg 91
31	Scripture Works for Pregnancy	Pg 94
32	Scripture Works for Protection/Safety	Pg 97
33	Scripture Works for Provision/Divine Supply	Pg 99
34	Scripture Works for Renewal of Youth	Pg 102
35	Scripture Works for Restoration	Pg 105
36	Scripture Works Revelation	Pg 107
37	Scripture Works for Salvation	Pg 109
38	Scripture Works for Spiritual Growth	Pg 111
39	Scripture Works for Thanksgiving & Praise	Pg 114

40	Scripture Works for Tithes & Offerings	Pg 116
41	Scripture Works for Victory	Pg 118
42	Scripture Works for Warfare & Breaking Curses	Pg 121
43	Scripture Works for Wisdom	Pg 125
44	Scripture Works for Wives	Pg 128
45	Scripture Works Daily Faith Declarations	Pg 131

PREFACE

*"...and you have magnified your **word above** all your name!" Psalm 138:2*

Over time in my walk with God, I have discovered and experienced the power of God released through praying his word, taking his promises back to him in prayers; by faith agreeing with what his word says concerning my situations; speaking and acting in line with his word. And God has never, and can never, fail to honor his word.

God will not deny his word. What he says he will do, is what he will do. *"God is not a man, that he should lie; neither the son of man, that he should repent: hath he said, and shall he not do it? or hath he spoken, and shall he not make it good?"* –Numbers 23:19. We are to *"...come boldly unto the throne of grace, that we may obtain mercy, and find grace to help in time of need."* Heb.4:16

We have so many promises of God in the bible, but we need to not only read them, but also meditate on them; and by faith, pray with them. As we do this, we will experience more of God's power in our lives. But why pray with the scriptures? You may ask. The word of God is powerful, it is alive! But even though we know the magnitude of God's word and power, it is our responsibility to express our needs and desires to him. *"For verily I say unto you, That whosoever shall say unto this mountain, Be thou removed, and be thou cast into the sea; and shall not doubt in his heart, but shall believe that those things which he saith shall come to pass; he shall have whatsoever he saith."* Mark 11:23

We may have a pen that writes perfectly well, for example. We may also need something to write with. But as long as that pen remains on our desk unused, it profits us nothing. No matter how much we desire for it to write and regardless of how much we need it to write, nothing happens...until we pick it up and use it. Likewise if I have a million dollar good check, it is not beneficial to me until I present it to the bank, and make withdrawals. We have "checks" from God in his word (promises) but we need to present our "checks" and make withdrawals in the place of scriptural praying. Praying God's word enables us to pray his will for our lives.

I love to pray the scriptures, it's powerful, it's exciting, and it's comforting knowing God cannot deny his word. *"For all the promises of God in him are yea, and in him Amen, unto the glory of God by us" 2 Corinthians 1:20.*

However, to fully enjoy these privileges in God, it is important that we have a relationship with him; and be in constant fellowship with him...after all we were created for his glory. We need to constantly abide in his presence and his word; and obey him...then it becomes real joy praying the scriptures as we see the results of our prayers!

Personally, I have come to know the power of praying his word when faced with diverse challenges and have discovered that scripture works! My desire is to share some of these powerful scriptures, and more, that have brought tremendous changes and victories to my life. My prayer is that you will be guided by the Holy Spirit to apply and pray the right scripture (God's word) over every situation in your life; and as you pray that you find relief, peace and answers to your life issues, in Jesus' name.

This book is a scripture praying reference and guide. My prayer is that the Lord himself embraces and minister to you as you pray the scriptures. It is my prayer that the Lord becomes real to you as you study His word and use this book as a scripture praying resource.

Remember, Scripture Works!

INTRODUCTION

Power of The Spoken Word
"Death and life are in the power of the tongue: and they that love it shall eat the fruit thereof." - Proverbs 18:21

Do you know there is a miracle in your mouth? Yes, right in your own mouth! If you knew your words shaped your life, and that what you say will come to pass, would you still speak the same kind of words? Take some time to consider what is coming out of your mouth. If your answer to the question above is no, then it's time for a change!

Because of my numerous experiences with the power in the word of God, I cannot but continually emphasize the role of scriptures in prayers. It grieves my heart that many Christians still have not tapped into this divine truth, and so many get frustrated in the place of prayer. They burn out after only few words, and are ready to quit the prayer session. My desire is that never again will you lack effective words to say to the Lord in your prayer time. Never again will you leave his presence unsure whether or not he heard you. But rather, confident that he heard and your prayers are answered.

We were created in the image and likeness of God (Genesis 1:27). We also know God created this world by the power of the spoken word. He said *"Let there be light..."* And there was! -Genesis 1. He has given us the same authority to create with our words - *"Verily, verily, I say unto you, He that believeth on me, the works that I do shall he do also; and greater works than these shall he do; because I go unto my Father."* John 14:12

Unfortunately, many have called only negative things into their lives, by continually speaking their fears and "reporting" their current unpleasant situations. This is contrary to God's desire for us. He says, in his word *"...let the weak say I am strong"* - *Joel 3:10*. We should, instead, dwell on what God is doing, and is about to do in our lives, shifting our gaze away from the problems, and focusing on his promises and plans for us - *"For I know the thoughts that I think toward you, saith the Lord, thoughts of peace, and not of evil, to give you an expected end."* - *Jeremiah 29:11*

A while back, I had so many things going on in my life at the same time. I had a new baby, a full time job with very long commute, was in school for my MBA, and had some volunteer work I was committed to. Needless to say, I was very stressed and didn't know what to do. I would return home on work days too late and too tired to do anything else. I had put school on hold for so long, and just returned, so opting out was not an option. But then I remembered a fellow Christian once testified on how he constantly declared "I live a stress-free life". So, I started to confess over my life: "I live a stress-free life, in the name of Jesus". I also prayed Matthew 11:28 *"come to me all you who are weary and burdened and I will give you rest"*. I'd declare "I receive rest, I am restful, I live a toil-free life, in Jesus' name"; and things began to change. I started to feel less stressed, and I got wisdom to manage my time more effectively. I generally started to enjoy life much more than I had in the past.

Another time, I had difficulty sleeping through the night; I started to pray Psalm 127: 2 and would declare "He gives his beloved sleep. I am his beloved, therefore I sleep soundly, and I'm well rested in Jesus' name..." Before long, I started to sleep well, and wake up refreshed the next morning! These are just two simple accounts out of several experiences I've had using the word of God in prayers. I have used the scriptures to pray jobs be created for me where there were no openings; I have used it to change jobs when I needed to. I have prayed the scriptures to find missing items and important documents. I have also used it to get clarity on issues. In fact, I have prayed scriptures on every area of my life. When I pray these scriptures, I always expect to get the desired result by faith, and God will always honor our faith! Indeed scripture works!

I want you to know that the same way God spoke words right from the beginning, we also can speak words over our lives, circumstances, work, loved ones...and the list goes on. And what better words to speak than God's own words? This is, simply put, praying the scriptures. When our prayers are based on the word of God, we pray his will. This way we have the guarantee that he hears us. *"This is the confidence we have in approaching God: that if we ask anything according to his will, he hears us"* – 1 John 5:14 (NIV).

Remember our God calls those things that be not as though they were (Romans 4:17). It is time for us to start acting like the God that created us in his image; moving our focus away from situations that are displeasing to us, but rather focusing on what can, and will be; based on his will for us, as found in his word, the Bible. It is time to take hold of his word, and speak them over our lives and situations...It is time! Are you ready?

Declare the Word of God - Speak it!

"Thou shalt also decree a thing, and it shall be established unto thee: and the light shall shine upon thy ways" – Job 22:28.

"For it is by believing in your heart that you are made right with God, and it is by confessing with your mouth that you are saved." – Romans 10:10 (NLT)

Someone rightly said a closed mouth is a closed destiny! We must begin to speak out the word of God over our lives, family and circumstances. It is not enough to know the word, read it, and practice it. When it comes to praying God's word over our lives, we must open our mouth and SPEAK! Even

God, our Maker, and the Creator of ALL things spoke things into existence. In Genesis 1, we see several accounts of God making declarations, commanding, speaking. *"God said..."* is a statement that is so common all through the bible; particularly in the story of creation.

So, what do you desire to create in your life? Do you desire a peaceful life, harmonious marriage, successful career, financial breakthroughs? Whatever it is, begin to speak faith-filled words, direct from the Bible. We see another account of God's desire for us to speak to situations and events in Mark 11:23, where we read, *"For verily I say unto you, That whosoever shall say unto this mountain, Be thou removed, and be thou cast into the sea; and shall not doubt in his heart, but shall believe that those things which he saith shall come to pass; he shall have whatsoever he saith."*

The Word of God as Seed

The word of God is seed (Luke 8:11) that we can plant in our hearts. We do this by spending time studying and meditating the Bible. We also plant these words by releasing them over our situations. When we plant God's words in our hearts, and situations, we are sure to get the desired harvest.

God's word works and can never fail. However, to get results, we must be willing to do whatever he tells us to do. This is important. In other words, "Word Practice" is paramount! We need to actually do what God commands us (obedience). Let's look at Peter's case in Matthew 17:27, for example. Jesus instructed him to "go" get money from the mouth of the fish. He had to do what Jesus told him, to get the promised outcome. You must practice the word, for it to bless your life.

This book, "Scripture Works!" is not about cramming scriptures, or muttering mere words, but rather strengthening of our spirit man by understanding the word of God, through the help of the Holy Spirit; and praying with purpose and the power of the Holy Ghost. Remember the letter alone has no power without the Holy Spirit *"Who also hath made us able ministers of the new testament; not of the letter, but of the spirit:* **for the letter killeth, but the spirit giveth life."** *-2 Corinthians 3:6*

Consistency is Key!

Have you noticed how many times we start off with good intentions, promising ourselves we will start certain disciplines, only to back out too soon? To experience the joy of answered prayers, we must be consistent in the place of prayer. We must also be consistent in speaking the scriptures over our lives and circumstances. We cannot afford to proclaim God's word in faith one day, and the next confess something to the contrary. It is very important to be consistent and refuse to give up, even if it looks like nothing is happening. Remember when Daniel prayed, his answer was dispatched the moment he prayed, but the king of Persia withheld the angel bringing the answer; but thank God Daniel persisted! - Daniel 10:1-14. Do not be weak in your days of adversity. Continue believing and trusting God for your miracle. Speak the favor of God, his protection, deliverance, grace…Speak his word over your life continually, habitually. *"And let us not be weary in well doing: for in due season we shall reap, if we faint not." -Galatians 6:9*

The Faith Part

Words without faith are mere empty words. Never forget to mix your words with faith in God. *"…but the word preached did not profit them, not being mixed with faith in them that heard it" – Hebrews 4:2. He replied, "Because you have so little faith. I tell you the truth, if you have faith as small as a mustard seed, you can say to this mountain, 'Move from here to there' and it will move. Nothing will be impossible for you." -Matthew 17:20 (NIV)*

Just as praying God's word guarantees us his audience (because he hears when we pray according to his will); our faith in him, his word and name, guarantees us the answer. We are to approach the throne of God boldly, in the name of Jesus, confident that he will grant us the desires of our hearts. *"And whatsoever ye shall ask in my name, that will I do, that the Father may be glorified in the Son. If ye shall ask any thing in my name, I will do it." – John 14:13-14.* Our faith in the name of Jesus is a requirement, and not an option, for answered prayers. *"Through faith in the name of Jesus, this man was healed--and you know how crippled he was before. Faith in Jesus' name has healed him before your very eyes." – Acts 3:16 (NLT)*

How then do we keep our faith alive, and believe the seemingly impossible? Testimonies are a great place to start. There are several accounts of God's mighty acts and deliverances in the Bible. The testimonies of others around us are also great faith boosters, and don't forget to recall his past acts of goodness in your own personal life. We often forget that many of the experiences we have are actually testimonies of God's love and faithfulness, and we sometimes fail to acknowledge and thank God for them; or to recount them when we are in need of our next miracle. Let's make conscious efforts to remember.

Boost your faith. Recount the different times in your life you saw the hand of God at work; both in your own life and that of others around you. When David was faced with Goliath, he recalled the testimonies of how he fought and killed the lion and the bear. This must have given him renewed strength and confidence - that if God did it with the lion and the bear, he would do it again with Goliath! And he sure prevailed!

Daily grow your faith (2 Thessalonians 1:3). Faith as small as a mustard seed is all you need to get started. Begin to exercise your faith in every area of your life; and as you do so, your faith will begin to grow. Even in the little things, exercise your faith; believe him for a good parking spot, for instance, for quick checkout at the grocery store...seemingly little things like that. As you see him come through in the little things in your life, it strengthens your faith and confidence in God; and before you know it, you will believe and trust him for, not just the bigger issues of your life, but everything!

Also spend time in the word of God; read about the miracles he performed, how he did the impossible; particularly in the areas you need his intervention. Make a habit of remembering the works of the Lord, in your life, in the reports of victory recorded in the bible, as well as in the lives of fellow believers that you have heard about. Be thankful for all of these praise reports; and because the bible is the truth, know for sure that Hebrews 13:8 is true! He is the same yesterday, today and forever! He is still in the business of performing miracles.

Never relent in your practice of believing him for everything. Remember we are to pray without ceasing, and prayer must always go hand-in-hand with faith to produce results. He has performed miracles in the past, answered prayers in the past, and He will do it again! *"Therefore I say unto you, What things soever ye desire, when ye pray, believe that ye receive them, and ye shall have them."* -Mark 11:24

If you believe you receive your petitions, then proclaim it in praise and thanksgiving. Let the faith in you be expressed through your thanksgiving, and acting like you got it already! Rejoice! Your faith will propel you into action. It will propel you into triumph! Like it made Noah start building an ark when it had never rained before (Hebrews 11:7), faith will propel you to prepare for what you have asked the Lord for, in anticipation of its manifestation. Faith will stabilize you and help you not to stagger at God's promises. It gives peace in the midst of challenges. It is daring and does not believe in impossibilities. It always wins!

The scriptural word content in our prayers and our faith will guarantee answers to our prayers. Approach God knowing that he is able and he is willing to help you. *'Jesus reached out his hand and touched the man. "I am willing," he said…'- Luke 5:13 (NIV)*

He is asking you today: *"Do you believe that I am able to do this?" (Matthew 9:28).* Believe! He will help you! *"For the Lord GOD will help me; therefore shall I not be confounded: therefore have I set my face like a flint, and I know that I shall not be ashamed" – Isaiah 50:7*

Observe Prayer Protocol

Enter into his gates with thanksgiving, and into his courts with praise: be thankful unto him, and bless his name. -Psalm 100:4

When you pray, always start and end your prayers with praise, adoration and worship of our God, the Most High. Remember our Lord Jesus showed us an example when he taught the disciples how to pray, *"This, then, is how you should pray: "'Our Father in heaven, hallowed be your name," -Matthew 6:9 (NIV)*

Make your requests known, "with thanksgiving" - Philippians 4:6. In other words, end your prayers thanking God.

Last but not the least, do you know him? Have you made him your Lord and Savior? You must have Jesus, to have access to the Father. *"Jesus saith unto him, I am the way, the truth, and the life: no man cometh unto the Father, but by me." -John 14:6.* If you don't have that relationship yet, pray the **"Salvation Prayer"** at the end of this book. *…for, "Everyone who calls on the name of the Lord will be saved." -Romans 10:13(NIV)*

How to Use this book

This book helps you prepare as you approach God in prayer; equipping you with appropriate verses for your prayer requests. Praying using God's word and promises is "bringing forth our strong reasons." (Isaiah 41:21). It is finding the right "keys" to open the door of our breakthroughs for that situation we are praying about. This book, **Scripture Works!** will give you practice of praying the scriptures, as well as show you how to turn any scripture that God puts in your heart, into prayers.

Scripture Works! can be used in your Individual/Personal prayer time. It can also be used in a group setting. **Scripture Works!** can be used primarily to find bible verses for praying about the different life issues featured in this book; but it can also be a great resource for finding scriptures for encouraging yourself, or others.

The prayers and scriptures in this book have been grouped into different life situations for ease in finding any topic you need scriptures and prayers on. I have attempted, in this book, to share some of the things I have done (or picked up along life's journey) that have worked for me in getting results to prayers. I strongly believe we have the responsibility to partner with God in seeing our prayers answered and desires met.

I have also included some "**Action Tips**" to support some of the prayer topics. However, these are just to give you ideas, and get you started on possible steps you can take in that particular situation. As you pray, listen for the Holy Spirit's direction. He will guide you to more specific actions you need to take for your current challenges. In some cases, your faith "work" may only be to arise and PRAY! The scriptures and prayers in this book are designed to help you to do just that! In others situations, you may need to take some more actions. As you spend time in the word of God, and scripture-based prayers, the Holy Spirit will guide and lead you. Be expectant. He will speak to you. *"Howbeit when he, the Spirit of truth, is come, he will guide you into all truth: for he shall not speak of himself; but* *whatsoever he shall hear, that shall he speak: and he will shew you things to come." -John 16:13*

May the Lord grant you the grace to persist and be victorious, in Jesus' name.

'May the Lord bless you and keep you. May the Lord smile down on you and show you his kindness. May the Lord answer your prayers and give you peace.' -Numbers 6:24-26 (ERV). In Jesus' name, AMEN!

XIII

~~1~~
SCRIPTURE WORKS FOR ABUNDANCE

The thief cometh not, but for to steal, and to kill, and to destroy: I am come that they might have life, and that they might have it more abundantly. -John 10:10

When we look all around us, we see abundance in everything God made. From the land, to the skies, to the seas; all of nature speaks of God's abundance. Our God can never run out. He has more than enough for every creature. He is not a God of lack. Christ said he came that we may have life, and abundantly too! (John 10:10). When he stepped into the widow of Zarephath's case in 1 Kings 17:7-16, the jar of flour kept multiplying, and the oil did not run dry. We see another proof in 2 Kings 4: 1-7 where the prophet's widow became a successful business woman from a jar of oil. The oil stopped only when she had no more vessels, so the limitation was set by man not God. Likewise when Jesus fed the 5000 men, plus women and children, there were leftovers! Get rid of every lack mentality, and replace it with thoughts of abundance.

Anchor Scriptures:
But as it is written, Eye hath not seen, nor ear heard, neither have entered into the heart of man, the things which God hath prepared for them that love him. -1 Corinthians 2:9

And ye shall eat in plenty, and be satisfied, and praise the name of the LORD your God, that hath dealt wondrously with you: and my people shall never be ashamed. -Joel 2:26

The LORD is my shepherd; I shall not want. -Psalm 23:1

Prayer:
Father, in the name of Jesus, I come boldly to you today declaring your abundance in my life. I believe your word that Christ came to give me abundant life, and so I receive God's abundance in my family, my finances, career, and every area of my life. I agree with your word today, and declare that eyes have not seen nor ears heard what you have prepared for me, because I love you. I eat in plenty and I am satisfied. I live in abundance, and will never be in want, because you are my Shepherd, my Provider. I praise you Lord because I will not be ashamed, as I enjoy your abundance and be a source of blessing to others. In Jesus' name I pray.

Declaration of Faith:
❖ *Thou preparest a table before me in the presence of mine enemies: thou anointest my head with oil; my cup runneth over.-Psalm 23:5*

Father, I declare that you are bringing honor into my life. You are bringing out the good that no one thought possible in my life. I have abundance, more than enough, overflowing; and I'm a blessing to others, in the name of Jesus.

❖ *You crown the year with a bountiful harvest; even the hard pathways overflow with abundance. —Psalm 65:11(NLT)*

In the name of Jesus, this year is a fruitful year for me. I receive a bountiful harvest on every kind of seed I sow this year. Everything that proved difficult for me in the past begins to overflow with abundance now. All impossibilities are turned into possibilities for me this year. I enjoy abundance in my life from henceforth.

Additional Scriptures:
Psalm 36:8; Psalm 37:11; Proverbs 3:10; Matthew 6:33; 2 Corinthians 9:8

~~2~~
SCRIPTURE WORKS FOR ASSURANCE

He that spared not his own Son, but delivered him up for us all, how shall he not with him also freely give us all things? -Romans 8:32

Are you dealing with doubts, struggling to convince yourself that God cares and will do as he has promised? Let not your heart be troubled! (John 14:1). God has never failed, and will not fail you. Have you ever observed a little child around his/her loving father? You cannot miss the air of confidence and security they carry when in the presence of their father. God is the best Father of all. He says if we, being evil, know how to give good gifts to our children, how much more our Heavenly Father! (Luke 11:13)

Anchor Scriptures:
...Surely I know that it shall be well with them that fear God, which fear before him -Ecclesiastes 8:12

And who is he that will harm you, if ye be followers of that which is good? - 1Peter 3:13

You will do everything you have promised; LORD, your love is eternal. Complete the work that you have begun. -Psalms 138:8 (GNT)

God is not a man, that he should lie; neither the son of man, that he should repent: hath he said, and shall he not do it? or hath he spoken, and shall he not make it good? -Numbers 23:19

Yea, though I walk through the valley of the shadow of death, I will fear no evil: for thou art with me; thy rod and thy staff they comfort me - Psalm 23:4

And we know that all things work together for good to them that love God, to them who are the called according to his purpose. -Romans 8:28

Prayer:
I know it is well with me because I fear the Lord, so I will not be afraid what man can do to me. I thank you Lord for no harm shall befall me because I trust in the Lord, my God. Father, I know you are faithful and you will do all that you have promised; for you are not a man that you should lie, nor the son of man that you should repent. Therefore, I hold fast to my profession of faith and I do not waver until my change comes. I thank you because I have the peace of God, and I rest in you, fully confident that you are working all things together for my good.

Declaration of Faith:
❖ *The LORD thy God in the midst of thee is mighty; he will save, he will rejoice over thee with joy; he will rest in his love, he will joy over thee with singing.* - Zephaniah 3:17

Yes indeed the Lord my God is with me, and is saving me with his mighty hands. He takes great delight in me, and he will quiet me with his love. My deeds and acts bring him joy all the days of my life, in Jesus' name.

❖ *Let us hold fast the profession of our faith without wavering; (for he is faithful that promised;)* Hebrews 10:23

I hold fast the profession of my faith without wavering; thank you Lord because you are faithful to bring your promises to pass in my life.

Additional Scriptures:
Romans 8:39; Psalm 4:3; Philippians 1:6; John 5:24; 1 John 5:15; 1 John 3:22; James 1:12

~~3~~
SCRIPTURE WORKS FOR THE BLESSING

And God blessed them, saying, Be fruitful, and multiply… -Gen 1:22

Beloved, I wish above all things that thou mayest prosper and be in health, even as thy soul prospereth. -3John 1:2

God's original plan is for us to be blessed, and he has not changed his mind! As a parent I know one of my greatest desires is to see my children prosper and live a blessed life, and I will do whatever is in my power to help and support them. However, it is left to my children to accept my help and advice. More than any earthly parent, God desires that we live a blessed and prosperous life, so much so that he sent his only son to die for us and reconnect us to the blessing of the Father. God has made provision for us, but we have to receive it by faith and follow his leading as he guides us on how to manifest his blessings in our lives.

Anchor Scriptures:
Deuteronomy 28:1-14

Prayer:
And it will come to pass, as I continually hearken diligently unto the voice of the LORD my God, to observe and to do all his commandments which he commands me, that the LORD my God will set me on high above all nations of the earth:

And all these blessings will come on me, and overtake me, as I consistently hearken unto the voice of the LORD my God.

Blessed will I be in the city, and blessed will I be in the field. Blessed will be the fruit of my body, and the fruit of my ground, and the fruit of my cattle, the increase of my kine, and the flocks of my sheep.
Blessed will be my basket and my store.
Blessed will I be when I come in, and blessed will I be when I go out.

The LORD will cause my enemies that rise up against me to be smitten before my face: they shall come out against me one way, and flee before me seven ways. The LORD will command the blessing upon me in my storehouses, and in all that I set my hand unto; and he will bless me in the land which the LORD my God has given me. The LORD will establish me a holy people unto himself, as he hath sworn unto me, as I keep the commandments of the LORD my God, and walk in his ways.

And all people of the earth will see that I am called by the name of the LORD; and they will be afraid of me. And the LORD will make me plenteous in goods, in the fruit of my body, and in the fruit of my cattle, and in the fruit of my ground, in the land which the LORD swore unto my fathers to give me.

The LORD will open unto me his good treasure, the heaven to give the rain unto my land in his season, and to bless all the work of my hand: and I will lend unto many nations, and I will not borrow.

And the LORD will make me the head, and not the tail; and I will be above only, and I will not be beneath; as I hearken unto the commandments of the LORD my God, which He commands me this day, to observe and to do them: And I will not go aside from any of the words which He command me this day, to the right hand, or to the left, to go after other gods to serve them.

In Jesus' name, I have prayed.

- Based on Deuteronomy 28:1-14

Declaration of Faith:

❖ *The blessing of the Lord, it maketh rich, and he addeth no sorrow with it. -Proverbs 10:22*

Father, I receive your blessing today. I declare that by your blessing, I am rich and I have no sorrow in my life, in Jesus' name.

❖ *Charge them that are rich in this world, that they be not highminded, nor trust in uncertain riches, but in the living God, who giveth us richly all things to enjoy; -1 Timothy 6:17*

In the name of Jesus, I enjoy the blessings of God in my life and I will not be arrogant as a result of it. I do not trust in uncertain riches, but my trust is in God alone.

Additional Scriptures:

3 John 1:2; Habakkuk 3:19; 2 Corinthians 9:8; Matthew 6:30-33; Exodus 23:25; Psalm 1:1

~~4~~
SCRIPTURE WORKS FOR BREAKTHROUGH

Behold, I will do a new thing; now it shall spring forth; shall ye not know it? I will even make a way in the wilderness, and rivers in the desert. -Isaiah 43:19

God is always making ways for His children. We see this happen often in the bible, and if we take the time to reflect on our lives, and "count our blessings", we will see many times God moved on our behalf. A prime example in the bible is the story of the children of Israel at the Red Sea, with the armies of Egypt behind them (Exodus 14). It was a most defining moment for them as the Red Sea gave way for them to walk on dry ground, yet swallowing up all their enemies. What a great God we serve! God will always make a way for us, if we believe. He will never permit anything that is too much for us come our way.

Anchor Scriptures:
Every valley shall be exalted, and every mountain and hill shall be made low: and the crooked shall be made straight, and the rough places plain: And the glory of the LORD shall be revealed, and all flesh shall see it together: for the mouth of the LORD hath spoken it. -Isaiah 40:4-5

I know your deeds. See, I have placed before you an open door that no one can shut. I know that you have little strength, yet you have kept my word and have not denied my name. - Revelation 3:8

Prayer:
Father, I thank you because you are the God of breakthroughs. I declare today that a way is being made for me, and I know what actions and steps to take in each situation. I decree that every mountains and hills on my path are made low, in the name of Jesus. Every valley in my life is exalted. My paths are made straight and every rough place in my life is now plain. I will not stumble, I will not fall. Thank you for opening doors unto me that no one can shut. I see opportunities and I take hold of them. I walk into my breakthroughs and manifest your glory in my life, and all flesh shall see it and glorify your name. I have divine ideas and inspirations and I am divinely connected. I BREAKTHROUGH, in the name of Jesus!

Declaration of Faith:
- ❖ In the name of Jesus! I will not lose heart nor grow weary. I will not faint in acting nobly and doing right, for in due time and at the appointed season I will reap. I do not loosen or relax my courage, nor faint -Based on Galatians 6:9 (AMP)

- ❖ *Behold, I will do a new thing; now it shall spring forth; shall ye not know it? I will even make a way in the wilderness, and rivers in the desert. Isaiah 43:19*

In the name of Jesus, I receive newness in my life. The Lord is making ways for me in every wilderness situation of my life. He is making rivers in the desert for me, refreshing my life.

Additional Scriptures:
Micah 2:13; 1 Corinthians 10:13; Psalm 56:9

Action Tips:
- ➢ Spend time in God's word, with expectation to get specific instructions.
- ➢ Journal whatever God lays on your heart.

- ➤ Pray about what you have written down, asking God to confirm it through his word.
- ➤ Whatever the Lord instructs you, do it. Don't try to analyze it. You have to act in faith, only be certain of what God is leading you to do.

~~5~~
SCRIPTURE WORKS FOR BUSINESS

But thou shalt remember the Lord thy God: for it is he that giveth thee power to get wealth, that he may establish his covenant which he sware unto thy fathers, as it is this day. -Deuteronomy 8:18

Without God, we can do nothing (John 15:5). There's nothing more powerful and productive in business than partnering with God; inviting him in, and handing our business over to him. God desires to bless the works of our hands. He is the one that teaches us to profit, so when we put him first in our business, he provides us with wisdom, protects our business, and prospers us.

Anchor Scriptures:

The Lord shall open unto thee his good treasure, the heaven to give the rain unto thy land in his season, and to bless all the work of thine hand: and thou shalt lend unto many nations, and thou shalt not borrow. -Deuteronomy 28:12

Thou hast enlarged my steps under me, that my feet did not slip. -Psalm 18:36

Then they willingly received him into the ship: and immediately the ship was at the land whither they went. -John 6:21

The wicked flee when no man pursueth: but the righteous are bold as a lion. -Proverbs 28:1

The steps of a good man are ordered by the Lord : and he delighteth in his way. -*Psalms 37:23*

Prayer:
(In this prayer, fill in the blanks, as appropriate)

Father, in the name of Jesus, I thank you for the desire you have placed in my heart to start my own business. Your word says we have not because we ask not, so I come boldly unto you in the name of your son Jesus Christ asking that you anoint me this day to prosper in the works of my hands. I ask you to bless my hands and handiwork. I also ask for the grace, ability and divine direction on opening and operating my _____ business. I ask, in the name of Jesus, that my business will be a great success, in Jesus' name. As Jesus entered the disciples' boat and they were immediately at the place they were going, I invite you Lord Jesus into this boat called (name of your business). Let this business be catapulted to greatness; blessing me the owner, my employees, customers and the community at large.

Thank you because you have given me the power to make wealth, in the name of Jesus. This day, I decree that (name of your business) is blessed, favored, prosperous and highly successful. The works of my hands are blessed and I render these services/products to clients effortlessly and without errors, or any problems. Wonderful and enjoyable clients are being drawn to this business in the name of Jesus.

(Name of business) grows rapidly in the name of Jesus, and I am a part of the solution to this economy, as I employ workers and pay them well in (name of business). I have direction and know what to do and when to do anything regarding this business. Father, I enthrone you Lord and King over this business. My steps are ordered of God. I have understanding, excellent knowledge and full insight into this business. Clients/customers are satisfied with my services/products and pay me promptly, in the name of Jesus. I will not, and cannot fail. In the name of Jesus, I make $_____ minimum annual gain with consistent growth and increase. I receive boldness from you Lord, because you told me I will be bold as a lion.

I reject every doubt, fear, unbelief and anxiety, in the name of Jesus. I receive the Spirit of boldness, love and a sound mind. The Lord is opening unto me his good treasure, the heaven gives rain to my land in his season, and the Lord blesses all the work of my hand; my business shall lend unto many nations, and shall not borrow.

I pray for enlargement of steps in my business, in the name of Jesus. Through my business many souls will see that with God, nothing shall be impossible; and as a result souls will be won unto you, scholarships awarded, jobs given to the unemployed and many more acts that bring glory to your name. Father, take the rein of this business and move it as you please. I thank you for provision and a debt-free business, constantly growing accounts, peace, joy and love. I love you Father, and bless your Holy name. Thank you for answered prayers. In Jesus' name I have prayed.

Declaration of Faith:
> ❖ *I can do all things through Christ which strengtheneth me – Philippians 4:13*

Father, I receive supernatural strength and insight for my business. I declare that I will not be weary or slothful. Thank you Lord that your strength is evident in this business.

> ❖ *When Isaac planted his crops that year, he harvested a hundred times more grain than he planted, for the LORD blessed him. –Genesis 26:12 (NLT)*

As I do business this year, I receive a hundredfold returns, for the Lord is blessing my business in Jesus' name.

Additional Scriptures:
Philippians 2:13; Psalm 1:3; Psalm 90:17

Action points:
> ➤ Profess God's blessing on your business daily.

- Analyze business' current state and where you want the business to be in, at least, a year's time.
- List all possible ways to reach that point in a year's time.
- Set goals, and break into individual months, weeks, and even daily. Remember to set Specific, Measurable, Attainable, Relevant and Time-based goals to avoid frustration.
- Go through, and pray over your goals every day.
- Take action.

~~6~~
SCRIPTURE WORKS FOR CAREER/WORK

He shall be like a tree planted by the rivers of water, that bringeth forth his fruit in his season; his leaf also shall not wither; and whatsoever he doeth shall prosper -Psalm 1:3

We can be exceptional in our career and work. We can stand out! That is what our Heavenly Father desires for us. He has given us the ability to be the best at what we do. We will have direction and success in our work and career as we are diligent, believing and trusting him. Just like Daniel consulted God when faced with a critical challenge in his career (Daniel 2:16-19), we too can approach God for help and solutions. When we do so, we will, like Daniel, succeed and emerge as the best.

Anchor Scriptures:
And the king communed with them; and among them all was found none like Daniel, Hananiah, Mishael, and Azariah: therefore stood they before the king. And in all matters of wisdom and understanding, that the king enquired of them, he found them ten times better than all the magicians and astrologers that were in all his realm. -Daniel 1:19, 20

Then this Daniel was preferred above the presidents and princes, because an excellent spirit was in him; and the king thought to set him over the whole realm. -Daniel 6:3

Forasmuch as an excellent spirit, and knowledge, and understanding, interpreting of dreams, and shewing of hard sentences, and dissolving of doubts, were found in the same Daniel, whom the king named Belteshazzar: now let Daniel be called, and he will shew the interpretation. -Daniel 5:12

But you are a shield around me, O LORD; you bestow glory on me and lift up my head. -Psalms 3:3 (NIV)

Ye are the light of the world. A city that is set on an hill cannot be hid. -Matthew 5:14

Now God had caused the official to show favor and compassion to Daniel -Daniel 1:9 (NIV)

Prayer:
Lord, I thank you for my career and job. Thank you for the opportunity you have given me, and for your provision through this job. Father, I pray that I stand out and excel in all that I set my hands unto. I receive an excellent spirit and knowledge like you gave to Daniel. In the name of Jesus, I have understanding and have the solutions to any problem I encounter in my career and on my job.

I am a shining example of the blessed of the Lord, as you fill me with wisdom, and bestow your glory on me. I thank you for lifting my head up, and making me a reference point for intelligence and brilliancy. I declare that I am favored by all around me, and I know how to conduct my affairs with grace and wisdom. I thank you Lord, because you are lifting me up in my career and making me the brightest and the best. In Jesus' name I pray.

Declaration of Faith
❖ *For the Lord God is a sun and shield: the Lord will give grace and glory: no good thing will he withhold from them that walk uprightly. -Psalm 84:11*

Lord, I walk in your grace today. I receive only good things in my life. In the name of Jesus, I will not walk in darkness or ignorance, but rather in the light. I walk uprightly before you all the days of my life. Your glory radiates over me, and I am protected from all evil on my job because you are my shield. Thank you, Father!

❖ *For promotion cometh neither from the east, nor from the west, nor from the south. Psalm 75:6*

I have favor with all those that will decide on my advancement, and they will favor me. I make progress on my job and career, in Jesus' name.

Additional Scriptures:
Deuteronomy 28:13; Philippians 4:13; 1 Samuel 2:7; Romans 8:31-32

Action Tips:
- Work as unto the Lord (Colossians 3:23)
- Avoid complaining about your work, or who you work for.
- Focus on what to be thankful for on your job, and give thanks.
- Be diligent and faithful; and God will reward you.

~~7~~
SCRIPTURE WORKS FOR CHILDREN
(Praying for your children)

Lo, children are an heritage of the LORD: and the fruit of the womb is his reward. -Psalm 127:3

What a blessing children are to any family! They are God's gift to us, and the greatest gift we can give to them is praying the word of God consistently over their lives. We all have children in our lives that we can sow the seed of prayers into. They may be our very own children, our nieces, nephews, neighbors, or students. Whoever they are to us, God is very pleased when we lift these ones before him in prayers. Let's build the foundation of their lives on scriptural prayers, and the word of God - *"Train up a child in the way he should go: and when he is old, he will not depart from it." -Proverbs 22:6*

Anchor Scriptures:
And all thy children shall be taught of the LORD; and great shall be the peace of thy children. -Isaiah 54:13

As the new heavens and the new earth that I make will endure before me," declares the Lord, "so will your name and descendants endure. (NIV) - Isaiah 66:22

And the LORD shall make thee the head, and not the tail; and thou shalt be above only, and thou shalt not be beneath; if that thou hearken unto the commandments of the LORD thy God, which I command thee this day, to observe and to do them: -Deuteronomy 28:13

Let no man despise your youth; but be an example of the believers, in word, in conduct, in love, in spirit, in faith, in purity. -1 Timothy 4:12

And he answered, "You shall love the Lord your God with all your heart and with all your soul and with all your strength and with all your mind, and your neighbor as yourself." -Luke 10:27

He that dwelleth in the secret place of the most High shall abide under the shadow of the Almighty. There shall no evil befall thee, neither shall any plague come nigh thy dwelling. -Psalms 91:1, 10

From henceforth let no man trouble me: for I bear in my body the marks of the Lord Jesus. -Galatians 6:17

Behold, I and the children whom the Lord hath given me are for signs and for wonders in Israel from the Lord of hosts, which dwelleth in mount Zion. -Isaiah 8:18

And Jesus increased in wisdom and stature, and in favour with God and man. -Luke 2:52

Blessed is the man that walketh not in the counsel of the ungodly, nor standeth in the way of sinners, nor sitteth in the seat of the scornful. But his delight is in the law of the Lord; and in his law doth he meditate day and night. -Psalms 1:1, 2

This book of the law shall not depart out of thy mouth; but thou shalt meditate therein day and night, that thou mayest observe to do according to all that is written therein: for then thou shalt make thy way prosperous, and then thou shalt have good success. Joshua 1:8

Prayer:
Father, I thank you that my children are taught of the Lord, and great is their peace. I pray that my descendants will forever be in your presence, basking in your love, faithfulness and glory. I declare, in the name of Jesus, that my children obey the commandments of the Lord; that they are the head,

not the tail. They are above only and never beneath. They are examples of believers, in words, conduct, love, spirit, faith and purity; and no one shall despise their youth. My children know and accept the Lord Jesus, as their Lord and Savior. They love the Lord and serve him with all their hearts and souls. They dwell in the secret place of the most high and abide under the shadow of the Almighty; therefore they are exempted from every evil.

According to the word of God, no evil shall befall my children and no plague shall come near them. No man shall trouble them, for they bear in their bodies the marks of the Lord Jesus Christ. My children are for signs and wonders. Their minds are alert. My children are holy. They prosper in the works of their hands; they continue to grow in wisdom and stature and in favor with God and man. My children are blessed. They walk not in the counsel of the ungodly; sit not in the seat of the scornful; and will not stand in the ways of the sinners.

My children delight in the law of the Lord. They constantly, consistently and tirelessly meditate on God's laws day and night. My children's ways are prosperous and they have good success in all they do, in Jesus' name.

Declaration of Faith:

❖ *Praise ye the Lord. Blessed is the man that feareth the Lord, that delighteth greatly in his commandments. His seed shall be mighty upon earth: the generation of the upright shall be blessed. -Psalms 112:1, 2*

My children are blessed. They delight greatly in God's commandments and obey them

According to his word, my seed shall be mighty upon the earth; therefore (child's name) is indeed mighty upon the earth, and his/her name is great. My generation is blessed, in Jesus' name.

❖ *But thus saith the Lord, Even the captives of the mighty shall be taken away, and the prey of the terrible shall be delivered: for I will contend with him that contendeth with thee, and I will save thy children. -Isaiah 49:25*

My children are saved from evil, ungodly peer pressures, ungodly friendships and relationships. They are delivered from any, and every, form of captivity of their spirits, souls and bodies, in Jesus' name.

Additional Scriptures:
Daniel 1:17; Numbers 23:23; Deuteronomy 7:12-15; Isaiah 54:17; 2 Timothy 4:18; Luke 10:19

Action Tips:
> ➢ For younger children, develop the habit of releasing the word of God over them as you bathe them, and prepare them for the day.
> ➢ For all ages, release blessings on your children as you see their photos at work, or in your home, or as they cross your mind during the day.
> ➢ Never utter a negative word over your child. Bless them always. As you correct them, pronounce what/how you want them to be. Remember what you speak over your child is powerful! Only speak life over them.

~~8~~
SCRIPTURE WORKS FOR COURAGE

Have not I commanded thee? Be strong and of a good courage; be not afraid, neither be thou dismayed: for the LORD thy God is with thee whithersoever thou goest. -Joshua 1:9

God's promise to us is never to leave nor forsake us. This knowledge gives us the confidence and courage we need to face anything that comes our way. Because God cannot lie, we know he is with us in every situation, and we will always come through triumphant.

Anchor Scriptures:
I can do all things through Christ which strengtheneth me. -Philippians 4:13

You will not have to fight this battle. Take up your positions; stand firm and see the deliverance the Lord will give you, O Judah and Jerusalem. Do not be afraid; do not be discouraged. Go out to face them tomorrow, and the Lord will be with you. -2 Chronicles 20:17 (NIV)

Be strong and courageous. Do not be afraid or terrified because of them, for the LORD your God goes with you; he will never leave you nor forsake you. -Deuteronomy 31:6 (NIV)

For God hath not given us the spirit of fear; but of power, and of love, and of a sound mind. -2 Timothy 1:7

As the Philistine moved closer to attack him, David ran quickly toward the battle line to meet him -1 Samuel 17:48 (NIV)

Prayer:
Father, in the name of Jesus, I declare today that I do all things through Christ who strengthens me. I am courageous and full of faith in the power and ability of my Lord, Jesus Christ. I refuse to be afraid or terrified, because I know the Lord is with me wherever I go. I declare that I stand firm, and I enjoy God's divine intervention. I embark on every project, every task, with courage and determination, and I will not fail, in the name of Jesus. I have a sound mind, and I do not fear. I am of good courage; my heart is strengthened in this situation, as I wait on the Lord for direction. I will not be moved by what I see, but rather by the word of God. As David was bold when he faced Goliath, I receive grace and anointing for boldness in every situation I encounter. In the name of Jesus, I have total victory. I thank you Lord for answers to my prayers.

Declaration of Faith:
❖ *"Don't be afraid," the prophet answered. "Those who are with us are more than those who are with them." -2 Kings 6:16 (NIV)*

Lord, I thank you that you are with me, so I reject the spirit of fear, in Jesus' name.

❖ *Ye are of God, little children, and have overcome them: because greater is he that is in you than he that is in the world -1 John 4:4*

The Greater One (Jesus) lives in me, I am not afraid. I receive the peace of God in my life today

Additional Scriptures:
Psalms 46:2; Deuteronomy 20:1; Psalms 27:14

~~9~~
SCRIPTURE WORKS FOR DEBT FREEDOM
(Debt Repayment, Forgiveness, Cancellation)

The rich ruleth over the poor, and the borrower is servant to the lender. -Proverbs 22:7
If the Son therefore shall make you free, you shall be free indeed. -John 8:36

God's will for us is to be free from debt. He wants us to be the lender, not the borrower. All through the bible, we see God relieving his people of debt, through divine favor, divine inspiration and ideas; divine visitation, divine provision, and many other ways. He is the Sovereign God, and can do all things. Regardless of the magnitude of your debt, God can, and wants to set you free.

What exact miracle do you believe him for? Do you believe he is able to do it? Yes, He IS able to do ALL things! Dare to believe him for your debt freedom. He is willing to help, and is faithful. Determine to be unshakable in your belief regardless of the bills and threats that keep coming at you. Take time to study how God delivered his own people from debt in the bible. He knows what is best for every situation. He may decide to give you ideas, businesses, inheritance, anything to bring you provision; so you can make enough to pay off your debts like he did with the widow in 2Kings 4:1-7. In this particular case, he divinely gave the widow a new business that not only paid all her debts, but gave her plenty more to live on.

In Matthew 17: 24-27, he supernaturally provided for Peter to pay his taxes. He can also cancel (forgive) your debts, like he did for the children of Israel in Exodus 14; where we see the record of the very first national debt cancellation! If he could wipe out the debt of every individual in an entire nation, in one night, surely your case is not too big for him. Even today, there are several testimonies of God miraculously canceling debts, or paying them off! He is the same and does not change (Hebrews 13:8).

He sure can get you out of debt too! No matter how huge the debt, don't try to figure out how God will do it. He has not asked you to figure it out, only believe, that's all he asks of you; and he will guide you on how to be debt free! Be free, in Jesus' name.

Anchor Scriptures:

Jesus answered and said unto them, Verily I say unto you, If ye have faith, and doubt not, ye shall not only do this which is done to the fig tree, but also if ye shall say unto this mountain, Be thou removed, and be thou cast into the sea; it shall be done. -Matthew 21:21

Because he hath set his love upon me, therefore will I deliver him: I will set him on high, because he hath known my name. He shall call upon me, and I will answer him: I will be with him in trouble; I will deliver him, and honor him. -Psalm 91:14-15

Owe no man any thing, but to love one another: for he that loveth another hath fulfilled the law. -Romans 13:8

Then the lord of that servant was moved with compassion, and loosed him, and forgave him the debt. -Matthew 18:27

For now will I break his yoke from off thee, and will burst thy bonds in sunder. -Nahum 1:13

Then He arose and rebuked the wind, and said to the sea, "Peace, be still!" And the wind ceased and there was a great calm. -Mark 4:39 (NKJV)

Prayer:
Father, in the name of Jesus, I repent of any unwise decisions I made in the past that brought me into debt. I thank you Lord because you are the God who gives us second chances, and corrects our mistakes. Today, I speak to the mountain of debt in my life: be gone in Jesus' name! I declare total freedom from every debt I owe. The yoke of indebtedness is broken off me and I am delivered and set free from the bondage of debt, in Jesus' name. I declare from henceforth I owe no man nothing but love.

I speak to every storm threatening my peace, as a result of debt: "Peace, be still" in Jesus' name. I declare I have the peace of God regarding this issue, and I experience calmness in my spirit, and my mind. I receive supernatural debt cancellation, forgiveness of debt; and restoration. I have supernatural money making ideas; and divine favor before God and man. I declare all my debts paid in full in the name of Jesus. The son has made me free, so I declare I am free indeed. I will not be bound by indebtedness anymore, in Jesus' name.

Declaration of Faith:
> ❖ *For God says, "At just the right time, I heard you. On the day of salvation, I helped you." Indeed, the "right time" is now. Today is the day of salvation. – 2 Corinthians 6:2 (NLT)*

The Lord has heard me today. He is helping me right now. Today is the day of my salvation from debt. He is working all things out for my good. I receive favor concerning every debt I owe, NOW, in the name of Jesus.

> ❖ *And Moses said unto the people, Fear ye not, stand still, and see the salvation of the LORD, which he will shew to you to day: for the Egyptians whom ye have seen to day, ye shall see them again no more for ever. –Exodus 14:13*

In the name of Jesus, the debt I see now, I will see them no more. I receive the peace of God. I will not be stuck in debt, I am going forward, and making progress.

❖ *And I will give this people favour in the sight of the Egyptians: and it shall come to pass, that, when ye go, ye shall not go empty:* -*Exodus 3:21*

I believe your word, and declare that I have and receive favor in the sight of all my creditors. I thank you that you are working behind the scenes to bring me favor beyond my wildest dreams, in Jesus' name.

❖ *And Jesus looking upon them saith, With men it is impossible, but not with God: for with God all things are possible.* -*Mark 10:27*

Thank you for making debt freedom a possibility in my life, and for making me a reference point for the power and miracle of God. With God all things are possible, including my debt freedom.

Additional Scriptures:
Joshua 1:8; Isaiah 43:18-19; Galatians 5:1; Malachi 3: 10-12; Matthew 6:33; Deuteronomy 15:6; Exodus 14:13-16; Luke 4:18

Action Tips: (The Holy Spirit will guide you on what specific actions to take in your peculiar situation. These are just some thoughts to get you started.)
- ➢ Know exactly how much you owe.
- ➢ List them out, and present them before the Lord when you pray. Mention the exact amounts.
- ➢ Prayerfully consider what options are available to you for these debts to be fully paid off. Listen for the leading of the Holy Spirit.
- ➢ Determine when you want this paid off. Based on you income, how feasible is your goal?
- ➢ How much can you put towards the payment yearly?

Break those into months, and then per paycheck.
- Consider what you can do for additional income…maybe something you're good at. Can you teach a language or skill, can you bake, paint, clean etc? Do you have something you don't need that you can sell for additional funds?
- Start somewhere, even if you believe for debt cancellation. Be faithful, pay your bills and be a good steward of whatever financial blessings God brings into your hands; and God will supernaturally move in to help you.
- Stay out of debt. Don't accumulate more debts.

~~10~~
SCRIPTURE WORKS FOR DELIVERANCE

Shall the prey be taken from the mighty, or the lawful captive delivered? But thus saith the LORD, Even the captives of the mighty shall be taken away, and the prey of the terrible shall be delivered: for I will contend with him that contendeth with thee, and I will save thy children. And I will feed them that oppress thee with their own flesh; and they shall be drunken with their own blood, as with sweet wine: and all flesh shall know that I the LORD am thy Saviour and thy Redeemer, the mighty One of Jacob. -Isaiah 49:24-26

Praise God, he is our Deliverer! He always was, and still is. There is none that is mighty to save as our God. He delivered the children of Israel (Exodus 14). He destroyed Goliath before the armies of Israel (1 Samuel 17). He delivered Daniel in the lion's den by shutting the mouth of the lions (Daniel 6). He delivered Joseph from slavery and made him Prime Minister instead (Genesis 41). He delivered Peter from the death row (Acts 12:5-17). What a Mighty God! Do you feel bound and it looks like there is no way out? Do you feel like you are being thrown to the lions to feast on? Are you physically or spiritually oppressed? Know for sure that *"...For this purpose the Son of God was manifested, that he might destroy the works of the devil." -1 John 3:8b*. Believe God for your deliverance as you lift your voice in prayers of faith.

Anchor Scriptures:
And Jesus came and spake unto them, saying, All power is given unto me in heaven and in earth. -Matthew 28:18

Behold, I give unto you power to tread on serpents and scorpions, and over all the power of the enemy: and nothing shall by any means hurt you. -Luke 10:19

Wherefore God also hath highly exalted him, and given him a name which is above every name: That at the name of Jesus every knee should bow, of things in heaven, and things in earth, and things under the earth;
And that every tongue should confess that Jesus Christ is Lord, to the glory of God the Father. -Philippians 2:9-11

Giving joyful thanks to the Father, who has qualified you to share in the inheritance of his holy people in the kingdom of light. For he has rescued us from the dominion of darkness and brought us into the kingdom of the Son he loves, -Colossians 1:12-13 (NIV)

He that committeth sin is of the devil; for the devil sinneth from the beginning. For this purpose the Son of God was manifested, that he might destroy the works of the devil. -1 John 3:8

For the oppression of the poor, for the sighing of the needy, now will I arise, saith the LORD; I will set him in safety from him that puffeth at him -Psalm 12:5

Behold, the days come, saith the LORD, that the plowman shall overtake the reaper, and the treader of grapes him that soweth seed; and the mountains shall drop sweet wine, and all the hills shall melt. -Amos 9:13

The LORD hath broken the staff of the wicked, and the sceptre of the rulers. -Isaiah 14:5

That I will break the Assyrian in my land, and upon my mountains tread him under foot: then shall his yoke depart from off them, and his burden depart from off their shoulders. -Isaiah 14:25

For the LORD of hosts hath purposed, and who shall disannul it? and his hand is stretched out, and who shall turn it back? -Isaiah 14:27

Prayer:
Father I thank you for the authority you have given me, as a believer, in the name of Jesus. I declare today that I am delivered from every form of captivity - spiritual, financial, physical or emotional. I believe I receive my liberty from every force contrary to the Spirit of God. I thank you because every work of the devil in my life is destroyed in the name of Jesus, for your word says this is the purpose that Jesus was manifested, to destroy the works of the devil. Therefore all works of the devil regarding my career, family, home, finances and other areas of my life are destroyed, in the name of Jesus. From this day on, I walk in the liberty wherewith Christ has made me free. The staff of the wicked, and the scepter of evil rulers of darkness in my life, is broken, in the name of Jesus! Christ has made me free, so I am free indeed.

I thank you, Lord, because I receive your power, and I tread on snakes and scorpions and over all the power of the enemy, and nothing shall by any means hurt me. Father, arise; deliver me from every oppression of the enemy. Keep me in safety from every attack of the evil one. Let every yoke be taken off me, and every burden removed from my shoulders. Lord, as you have purposed to deliver me, none shall annul it; as you have stretched out your hand of salvation to me, none can turn it back.

And now, I take authority over every power of darkness around me in the name of Jesus. I bind you and command you OUT of my life, family, finances, and everything that concerns me. I destroy your works in my life; and render your power over me and mine null and void, in the name of Jesus!

Thank you Lord because now I am delivered from the power of darkness and translated into the kingdom of God, in Jesus' name.

Declaration of Faith:
❖ *For now will I break his yoke from off thee, and will burst thy bonds in sunder. -Nahum 1:13*
Every yoke is broken off me; and I am delivered from all

bondage in Jesus' name.

> ❖ *The Lord your God is with you, he is mighty to save. He will take great delight in you, he will quiet you with his love, he will rejoice over you with singing. -Zephaniah 3:17 (NIV)*

I enjoy the peace and quietness of God, and I will always have reasons to praise him, in Jesus' name.

> ❖ *But the salvation of the righteous is of the LORD: he is their strength in the time of trouble. -Psalms 37:39*

God is my strength in trouble, and the deliverer of my soul.

> ❖ *Ye that love the LORD, hate evil: he preserveth the souls of his saints; he delivereth them out of the hand of the wicked - Psalm 97:10*

I love the Lord and hate evil, therefore the Lord preserves my soul. He delivers me from the hand of the wicked, in Jesus' name.

Additional Scriptures:
Matthew 15:13; Galatians 3:13-14; 2 Samuel 22:45-46; Proverbs 26:2; Numbers 23:23; 2 Timothy 4:18

~~11~~
SCRIPTURE WORKS FOR EMPLOYMENT INTERVIEW

For the Holy Ghost shall teach you in the same hour what ye ought to say. - Luke 12:12

The Holy Ghost is our Helper, and our Teacher. He knows all things. If we rely on Him, He'll guide us through life, letting us know when to speak, what to say, and when to simply be quite and listen. Our Father God is interested in every area of our lives. He wants us to be the very best, for his glory. He made Daniel and his friends ten times better when they were interviewed (Daniel 1:20); and they got the positions! The Holy Spirit will fill you with wisdom from God. He will make you far better than all others, and preferred, in Jesus' name.

Anchor Scriptures:
Now God had brought Daniel into favour and tender love with the prince of the eunuchs.

As for these four children, God gave them knowledge and skill in all learning and wisdom: and Daniel had understanding in all visions and dreams.

And the king communed with them; and among them all was found none like Daniel, Hananiah, Mishael, and Azariah: therefore stood they before the king.

And in all matters of wisdom and understanding, that the king enquired of them, he found them ten times better than all the magicians and astrologers that were in all his realm. - Daniel 1:9, 17, 19-20

I am the Lord thy God, which brought thee out of the land of Egypt: open thy mouth wide, and I will fill it. - Psalm 81:10

So then it is not of him that willeth, nor of him that runneth, but of God that sheweth mercy. - Romans 9:16

So God will choose anyone he decides to show mercy to, and his choice does not depend on what people want or try to do. - Romans 9:16 *(ERV)*

Prayer:
Father, in the name of Jesus, I thank you for the opportunity to interview at (company's name). I stand on your word and ask for favor with the hiring manager, and any other person that will make decisions regarding this position (mention position). As Daniel found favor before the prince of the eunuchs, so may I find favor before all that I come in contact with during this hiring process. I pray for the Spirit of Wisdom to rest on me, and for the Holy Spirit to teach me what I ought to say, and that my mouth be filled with the right words each time I speak.

I pray that I am relaxed, and genuine; that in all that will be enquired of me, I will be found ten times better than all others that are being interviewed for this position. Lord, may your mercy prevail over my life and my career, in Jesus' name. I thank you Lord and I receive this job, as it is the desire of my heart. I thank you for a smooth and enjoyable interview, and for positive outcomes, in the name of Jesus. I thank you that as I receive and start this position, I will continually be the best. In Jesus mighty name I pray.

Declaration of Faith:
❖ *I can do all things through Christ which strengtheneth me. Philippians 4:13*

In Jesus' name I am not intimidated, I receive calmness and I do all things right, through Christ.

❖ *The king's heart is in the hand of the LORD, as the rivers of water: he turneth it whithersoever he will. Proverbs 21:1*

Thank you Lord, for you are turning the heart of the hiring manager in my favor, in Jesus name.

Additional Scriptures:
Psalm 34:10; Ephesians 4:28; Psalm 30:5

~~12~~
SCRIPTURE WORKS FOR ENLIGHTENMENT, DIRECTION & GUIDANCE

Howbeit when he, the Spirit of truth, is come, he will guide you into all truth: for he shall not speak of himself; but whatsoever he shall hear, that shall he speak: and he will shew you things to come. -John 16:13

When in need of direction and clarity, when faced with situations we are unsure of, or when life is meaningless [without form], and void, God invites us to come to him and he will lead and guide us in the path to go.

Anchor Scriptures:
And the earth was without form, and void; and darkness was upon the face of the deep. And the Spirit of God moved upon the face of the waters. And God said, Let there be light: and there was light. And God saw the light, that it was good: and God divided the light from the darkness. - Genesis 1:2-3

My sheep hear my voice, and I know them, and they follow me: -John 10:27

Behold, I send an Angel before thee, to keep thee in the way, and to bring thee into the place which I have prepared. -Exodus 23:20

Prayer:
Father, in the name of Jesus, I ask that your Spirit move over my life; I command every darkness to be dispelled from my life. I speak to my life and any situation in the dark in my life right now: "Let there be light!" in Jesus' name. I speak the glory light of God over my life, my marriage, my family, my career, my mind, my spirit, my soul and all of my

circumstances, in the name of Jesus.

I command anything in the dark in my life to begin to receive the light of God, in Jesus' name. I hear the voice of God, and I know it. I have clarity on what to do, in the name of Jesus. I receive solutions to any problem I am faced with. I receive insight and direction. Thank you Lord that your angel goes before me, and keeps me in the way; your angel brings me to the place you have prepared for me. All confusion disappears and I get clear guidance, in Jesus' name.

Declaration of Faith:

> ❖ *And thine ears shall hear a word behind thee, saying, This is the way, walk ye in it, when ye turn to the right hand, and when ye turn to the left. -Isaiah 30:21*

Father I thank you for your angel goes before me. I receive direction, I know the right way, and I walk in it. I turn not to the right or to the left. I am obedient and trust you, Lord. In Jesus' name I pray.

> ❖ *Trust in the Lord with all thine heart; and lean not unto thine own understanding. In all thy ways acknowledge him, and he shall direct thy paths. -Proverbs 3:5, 6*

Lord, I trust you and hand this situation over to you. I receive your leading, and come against every form of confusion. Thank you for directing my paths to take the right decisions for my situation, in Jesus' name.

Action Tips:

> ➢ Get alone with God, and spend time in the word of God, expecting him to speak specifically to you on the issue at hand.
>
> ➢ Jot down whatever he lays in your heart, and confirm with scriptures.
>
> ➢ Don't rush. Wait for more confirmation from the Lord - "…In the mouth of two or three witnesses shall every word be established." 2 Corinthians 13:1

~~13~~
SCRIPTURE WORKS FOR FAITH

But I have prayed for thee, that thy faith fail not: and when thou art converted, strengthen thy brethren. -Luke 22:32

You may wonder, "can we pray to have faith?" I believe we can. You need your faith alive because faith is what connects you with the power of God. It brings about a turnaround for you, and God's supernatural manifestation. Sometimes we feel like we simply cannot go on believing, or we face a situation that looks just impossible, so impossible that we feel our faith failing; and we, on the verge of giving up. Remember Jesus prayed for Peter that his faith fail not (Luke 22:32). We can pray same for ourselves and others; and experience supernatural strengthening of our inner man; keeping us believing, trusting, and against hope, having hope!

Anchor Scriptures:
And being not weak in faith, [Abraham] considered not his own body now dead, when he was about an hundred years old, neither yet the deadness of Sarah's womb: He staggered not at the promise of God through unbelief; but was strong in faith, giving glory to God. - Romans 4:19-20

For surely there is an end; and thine expectation shall not be cut off. -Proverbs 23:18

Now unto him that is able to do exceeding abundantly above all that we ask or think, according to the power that worketh in us. -Ephesians 3:20

Therefore I tell you, whatever you ask for in prayer, believe that you have received it, and it will be yours. -Mark 11:24 (NIV)

For with God nothing shall be impossible. -Luke 1:37

Prayer:
Father, in the name of Jesus, I receive the Spirit of Faith, such as was in Abraham. In the name of Jesus, I believe the word of God and act in obedience to all that you have commanded me. I am not moved by situations and circumstances around me, but rather by the word of God. I consider not my circumstances, and stagger not at the promises of God. I am strong in faith and give glory to God at all times. I believe you Lord, that my expectations shall not be cut off, and that you are able to do exceeding abundantly above all that I ask or think, according to the power of God that works in me. I believe you that each time I ask of you, I receive. I am a person of faith, and I do not waver. I thank you that my faith will not fail, in Jesus' name, Amen.

Declaration of Faith:
- *And the Lord said, If ye had faith as a grain of mustard seed, ye might say unto this sycamine tree, Be thou plucked up by the root, and be thou planted in the sea; and it should obey you. -Luke 17:6*

Lord I believe that as I speak to every seemingly impossible situation in my life; I begin to see results, in Jesus' name. (Now begin to speak, in faith, to every situation in your life that looks impossible, and command a supernatural change. God has given you authority!)

- *(For we walk by faith, not by sight:) -2 Corinthians 5:7*

In the name of Jesus, I consistently walk by faith and I'm not moved by what I see, but rather by the word of God

Additional Scriptures:
Matthew 6:30; John 11:40; Matthew 17:20; Habakkuk 2:4; Matthew 9:29; Mark 5:34

Action Tips:
- ➢ Surround yourself with the word of God. Listen to faith-filled music and messages. Faith comes by hearing, and hearing by the word of God – Romans 10:17
- ➢ Shut off any source of negativity, doubt or fear. If watching particular programs on TV, for example, fill you with wrong thoughts; then cut such off.
- ➢ Hang around people that speak and act faith sincerely; people that truly love the Lord.
- ➢ Be thankful. Find something to be grateful for in all situations, and give thanks.
- ➢ Recall past testimonies of God's faithfulness and power.
- ➢ Cultivate the habit of speaking positively only. Speak in line with God's promises for you!

~~14~~
SCRIPTURE WORKS FOR FAVOR

"And Jesus increased in wisdom and stature, and in favour with God and man."-Luke 2:52

The favor of God will open any door! When our ways please the Lord, he favors us so much so that even our enemies will be at peace with us (Proverbs 16:7). The favor of God will make ways for us, it will place us in positions we never thought possible. God's favor is what promotes us, and brings honor to our lives. The favor of God on our lives will cause men to give glory to God. It will even draw men to seek the God that we serve. It is time for the favor of God to be manifested in your life!

Anchor Scriptures:
For thou, LORD, wilt bless the righteous; with favour wilt thou compass him as with a shield. -Psalms 5:12

And I will give this people favour in the sight of the Egyptians: and it shall come to pass, that, when ye go, ye shall not go empty: -Exodus 3:21

Thou shalt arise, and have mercy upon Zion: for the time to favour her, yea, the set time, is come. -Psalms 102:13

For they got not the land in possession by their own sword, neither did their own arm save them: but thy right hand, and thine arm, and the light of thy countenance, because thou hadst a favour unto them. -Psalms 44:3

Prayer:
Father, in the name of Jesus, I thank you for your favor over my life. I declare this day that I increase in favor with God and with man. I am the righteousness of God in Christ Jesus; therefore I am blessed of the Lord. The favor of God surrounds and protects me like a shield. Lord, I thank you that as you gave the Israelites favor before the Egyptians, so also are you granting me favor before everyone and organization that you have purposed to be a blessing to me. Today is my set time for the favor of God, and my God is arising to favor me. In the name of Jesus, God's favor is so strong on my life; it brings me freedom, prosperity, abundance, peace and love. It changes rules in my favor, and battles are won which I do not have to fight. Thank you Lord for your undeniable favor and grace that is evident in my life! In Jesus' name I pray.

Declaration of Faith:
❖ *Remember me, O Lord, with the favour that thou bearest unto thy people: O visit me with thy salvation; -Psalms 106:4*

❖ *Thou hast granted me life and favour, and thy visitation hath preserved my spirit. Job 10:12*

Additional Scriptures:
Psalm 30:5; Psalm 90:17; Psalm 84:11; Genesis 39:4

Action Tips:
- Be kind and sow "favor seeds" into the lives of others. Remember what a man sows, he reaps (Galatians 6:7)
- Declare the favor of God over your life daily.
- Expect God's favor always.

~~15~~
SCRIPTURE WORKS FOR FINANCIAL INCREASE/PROSPERITY

Then Isaac sowed in that land, and received in the same year an hundredfold: and the Lord blessed him. -Genesis 26:12

When God created man, he said, "Be fruitful, and multiply..." Gen 1:28. Part of his will for our lives is increase. His word says the path of the righteous shines more and more (Proverbs 4:18). He also desires for us to prosper and be in good health (3 John 1:2). Our Father, God, desires to give us all things richly to enjoy (1 Timothy 6:17). We are to boldly believe and declare his promises for our financial increase and prosperity, in agreement with his word.

Anchor Scriptures:
"Give, and it shall be given unto you; good measure, pressed down, and shaken together, and running over, shall men give into your bosom. For with the same measure that ye mete withal it shall be measured to you again." -Luke 6:38

I wisdom dwell with prudence, and find out knowledge of witty inventions. -Proverbs 8:12

I know thy works: behold, I have set before thee an open door, and no man can shut it: for thou hast a little strength, and hast kept my word, and hast not denied my name. -Revelation 3:8

The Lord shall increase you more and more, you and your children. -Psalms 115:14

Wealth and riches shall be in his house: and his righteousness endureth for ever. -Psalms 112:3

And I will make of thee a great nation, and I will bless thee, and make thy name great; and thou shalt be a blessing: -Genesis 12:2

When men are cast down, then thou shalt say, There is lifting up; and he shall save the humble person. –Job 22:29

Prayer:

Father, in the name of Jesus, I call forth your blessing into our lives. Your word says you will cause men to give into our bosom. Lord, we tithe, and are givers; so in the name of Jesus, men are giving unto our bosoms according to your word. The Favor of God is mighty upon our lives. We are full of divine ideas, inspirations and witty inventions that bring us contracts, houses, cars, opportunities, and financial increase. We are constantly been paid huge sums of money for our work, creativity and even hobbies. Doors are opening unto us. Money comes to us easily and we are never without sufficient income and resources. We live stress-free, toil-free, debt-free lives.

We enjoy God's abundance and provision every day of our lives. We are faith people and believe easily without struggles. We see results as we believe and act in faith. Ideas are flooding our hearts, and God is connecting us with the right sources to materialize our ideas. We are blessed to be a blessing. We instantly and constantly see results in our lives, and the unbelievers envy us, as they envied Isaac. We increase in the recession. When men are saying there is a casting down, we declare and experience a supernatural lifting up, in the name of Jesus.

Declaration of Faith:

❖ *Bring ye all the tithes into the storehouse, that there may be meat in mine house, and prove me now herewith, saith the*

> *LORD of hosts, if I will not open you the windows of heaven, and pour you out a blessing, that there shall not be room enough to receive it. And I will rebuke the devourer for your sakes, and he shall not destroy the fruits of your ground; neither shall your vine cast her fruit before the time in the field, saith the LORD of hosts. —Malachi 3:10-11*

In the name of Jesus, every devourer in my life is rebuked, because I bring all my tithes into God's storehouse. By the power of the Holy Spirit, I come against every plan of the devil in my life. I decree that my fruits will not be destroyed, and the good things in my life shall not be aborted, in Jesus' name.

Additional Scriptures:
Deuteronomy 15:6; Ecclesiastes 3:13; Psalm 1:3; Psalm 35:27; Isaiah 58:11

Action Tips:
- Declare the blessings of God over your life daily.
- Spend time meditating on the word of God, and listening for God-given ideas.
- Journal ideas or impressions that come to mind (Write the vision)
- Prayerfully consider which of these ideas you can start working on.
- Determine what steps you need to take.
- Set attainable goals and plan on how to bring the vision to pass.
- Work your plan...with God all things are possible!

~~16~~
SCRIPTURE WORKS FOR FORGIVENESS

If my people, which are called by my name, shall humble themselves, and pray, and seek my face, and turn from their wicked ways; then will I hear from heaven, and will forgive their sin, and will heal their land. - 2 Chronicles 7:14

Our God is a merciful God. He is loving and forgiving. He assures us that when we confess our sins, he is faithful and just to forgive us (1 John 1:9). Do not be deceived into believing God will not forgive you. If you truly repent, he will forgive you. Therefore, forgive yourself and come out of condemnation, because God sent his son to the world not to condemn us, but to save us (John 3:17)

Anchor Scriptures:
If we confess our sins, he is faithful and just to forgive us our sins, and to cleanse us from all unrighteousness. -1 John 1:9

Come now, and let us reason together, saith the LORD: though your sins be as scarlet, they shall be as white as snow; though they be red like crimson, they shall be as wool. -Isaiah 1:18

All that the Father giveth me shall come to me; and him that cometh to me I will in no wise cast out. -John 6:37

I acknowledge my sin unto thee, and mine iniquity have I not hid. I said, I will confess my transgressions unto the LORD; and thou forgavest the iniquity of my sin. Selah. -Psalms 32:5

And I will cleanse them from all their iniquity, whereby they have sinned against me; and I will pardon all their iniquities, whereby they have sinned, and whereby they have transgressed against me. -Jeremiah 33:8

Prayer:
Father, I thank you for the blood of Jesus. Thank you that through the blood I have access to your throne room. I come now asking for the forgiveness of my sins. I believe your word that when I come unto you I will not be cast out. I ask that you forgive me for every way I have grieved your Holy Spirit. I humbly confess my sins and shortcomings. (Mention any specifics that the Holy Spirit lays on your heart, and ask for forgiveness). I thank you because you are faithful and just to forgive me my sins and cleanse me from all unrighteousness. Thank you for pardoning all my iniquities. I live free and liberated, free from sin and condemnation. Thank you Jesus!

Declaration of Faith:
❖ *Stand fast therefore in the liberty wherewith Christ hath made us free, and be not entangled again with the yoke of bondage. –Galatians 5:1*

Christ has made me free, and I will not be entangled with sin again. In Jesus' name, I am free from bondage.

❖ *Who shall lay any thing to the charge of God's elect? It is God that justifieth. –Romans 8:33*

I am God's elect, and I'm justified by God and the blood of his son Jesus Christ.

Additional Scriptures:
Proverbs 28:13; Isaiah 43:25; 2 Peter 3:9

~~17~~
SCRIPTURE WORKS FOR GAINFUL EMPLOYMENT

The Lord God took the man and put him in the Garden of Eden to work it and take care of it. -Genesis 2:15 (NIV)

Work was designed by our Heavenly Father; for us to engage with the earth he created for us; and for us to add value to it. It was never intended to be laborious and painful. Work was originally created to be enjoyed, and to be our service to our God. This is still what God intends, and we can live in his original plan and purpose. In addition, work was never intended to be our source - only God is our Source. Our work is the assignment that God has given us at a point in time, and is a resource he is using to bless us, so we can bless others. It must not take God's place in our lives.

Because God wants us to enjoy our work, he will give us gainful, enjoyable work if we believe him for it. If you are currently unemployed, believe God for your daily bread, he never fails. I once was laid off and without a job for a couple of years, but never was there a day of lack, because I trusted God as my Provider! He came through always, and met EVERY need (and even tipped it off with some wants too!). He is a good Father. He will give you his peace as you await your next assignment. Don't be discouraged, he has the best in store for you, and is never late. Just fix your gaze on him, and keep your hope in him alive. He will always come through, only trust him.

Anchor Scriptures:
But he said to them, "My Father never stops working, and so I work too." -John 5:17 (ERV)

Let not your heart be troubled: ye believe in God, believe also in me. -John 14:1

Let him that stole steal no more: but rather let him labour, working with his hands the thing which is good, that he may have to give to him that needeth. -Ephesians 4:28

I know thy works: behold, I have set before thee an open door, and no man can shut it: for thou hast a little strength, and hast kept my word, and hast not denied my name. -Revelation 3:8

Behold, I will do a new thing; now it shall spring forth; shall ye not know it? I will even make a way in the wilderness, and rivers in the desert. -Isaiah 43:19

A man's gift maketh room for him, and bringeth him before great men. -Proverbs 18:16

And I say unto you, Ask, and it shall be given you; seek, and ye shall find; knock, and it shall be opened unto you. -Luke 11:9

Prayers:
In the name of Jesus, Father I thank you for your word regarding employment. I thank you because it is your will for me to be gainfully employed, to work with my hands that which is good and honorable, so I can be a blessing to those in need. Father, this is my desire. I pray for open doors that no man can shut. I pray for a work that I will enjoy; work that will give me the opportunity to be a witness for you. I pray that you will make a way where there seem to be no way; causing there to be job creations where there were no vacancies. In the name of Jesus, I pray that my skills and personality will be needed and sought after. I cover my

resumes in the blood of Jesus, and pray that your favor will accompany every resume and application I send.

    I call forth my miracle job today, in the name of Jesus. My gifts, talents, personality and disposition make room for me this day, in Jesus' name. I thank you, because I have asked according to your word, and therefore receive my petitions. As I seek a new assignment, I find one speedily to the glory of your name. As I knock on company "doors" through my applications, interviews and other means, doors of favor and great job opportunities shall be opened unto me. I have my job; it physically manifests in the name of Jesus. Lord I receive your peace during this process. I will not be anxious but will continue to believe you for my miracle. Thank you, Jesus!

Declaration of Faith

But my God shall supply all your need according to his riches in glory by Christ Jesus. -Philippians 4:19

    In the name of Jesus, my need for employment is met, and I have no lack whatsoever while I wait for the manifestation.

If ye shall ask any thing in my name, I will do it. -John 14:14

Thank you faithful God, that when I ask anything in your name you will do it. I ask for a new job (give specifics on what kind of job, distance, hours, pay etc); and I thank you because I believe I receive my miracle job, in Jesus' name.

Additional Scriptures:
3 John 1:2; Joshua 1:8

Action Tips:
- Spend this time developing a closer walk with God. Keep a schedule for meeting with him daily.
- Volunteer your service, if you can.
- Check online and newspapers for training and other resources available to the unemployed.
- Seek and you shall find. Keep prayerfully looking

and sending your resumes in.
- What can you do while you're waiting for your next assignment? Can you teach a foreign language? Can you fix computers? Can you write? Can you start a business? List your skills and let people know you are available to offer these services at a token, you'll be amazed at what doors will be opened to you. Only chose something that will not drain money from you - beware of scams, and pray over everything you do. Be led by the Holy Spirit.

~~18~~
SCRIPTURE WORKS FOR GIFTS AND TALENTS

A man's gift maketh room for him, and bringeth him before great men. -Proverbs 18:16

Every one of us is blessed with a special talent or gift; and the Giver expects us to use these for his glory (Matthew 25:14-30). However, we often don't recognize these talents as our gifts and would sometimes overlook them, craving someone else's gifts and talents. Some do know and embrace their talents, but then are challenged with how to fully utilize these gifts to the glory of God; and not be distracted by the other demands of life. Finding fulfillment and purpose through your talent is possible. God will help us as we submit to him, and seek to please him first.

Anchor Scriptures:

As each of you has received a gift (a particular spiritual talent, a gracious divine endowment), employ it for one another as [befits] good trustees of God's many-sided grace [faithful stewards of the extremely diverse powers and gifts granted to Christians by unmerited favor]. -1 Peter 4:10 (AMP)

Wherefore I put thee in remembrance that thou stir up the gift of God, which is in thee by the putting on of my hands. -2 Timothy 1:6

Every good gift and every perfect gift is from above, and cometh down from the Father of lights, with whom is no variableness, neither shadow of turning. -James 1:17

Do not neglect the gift which is in you, [that special inward endowment] which was directly imparted to you [by the Holy Spirit] by prophetic utterance when the elders laid their hands upon you [at your ordination]. -1 Timothy 4:14 (AMP)

For the gifts and calling of God are without repentance.-Romans 11:29

Prayer:
Father, I thank you for the gifts and talents you have placed in me. In the name of Jesus, I receive the grace to stir up my gifts and talents. I receive direction and divine inspiration in manifesting the gifts of God in me. I declare that my gifts and talents are blessing me and all those around me. According to your word, my gifts make room for me, and bring me before great men. My gifts are creating opportunities for me, and I am divinely connected with the right people and resources, in the name of Jesus. Because every perfect gift is from you, I declare that my gifts and talents are perfect, in Jesus' name.

I receive all I need to polish and make my gifts and talents exceptional. I thank you because you are providing the training, mentorship, connections and whatever else I need for my gifts and talents to be excellent, and in demand. I thank you that my gifts from God are permanent, so I declare that any gift or talent I have overlooked, or made dormant, begins to be relevant and useful in my life. Doors are opening unto me to use my talents to bless mankind, in the name of Jesus. I amaze the world, as my talents are being unleashed, in the name of Jesus. Men are praising God as a result of my gifts and talents, in the name of Jesus.

Declaration of Faith:
❖ *So whether you eat or drink or whatever you do, do it all for the glory of God. -1 Corinthians 10:31 (NIV)*

Father, I declare in the name of Jesus, that whatever I do

with my talents will be for the glory of God.

Additional Scriptures:
Exodus 31:3-6; Psalm 18:33-34; 1 Corinthians 7:7; Romans 12:6

Action Tips:
- Identify what you enjoy doing most, what comes natural to you.
- Consider how you can improve this gift.
- Start using your talent. You can exercise your gift through volunteer work, for example. Remember practice makes perfect.
- Be diligent in whatever doors the Lord opens for you, and do not despise the days of little beginnings. As you are diligent, the Lord will reward your faithfulness, and open even more doors.

~~19~~
SCRIPTURE WORKS FOR HEALING

But he was wounded for our transgressions, he was bruised for our iniquities: the chastisement of our peace was upon him; and with his stripes we are healed. -Isaiah 53:5
He sent his word, and healed them, and delivered them from their destructions. -Psalm 107:20

It's a no-brainer that Jesus wants us whole and complete. He wants us to enjoy good health. The devil may bring deception through symptoms, which may be facts, but the truth of the word of God will overcome every symptom and make us triumph each time! What is this truth? The truth is that by his stripes we were healed; the truth is that he suffered so we would not have to; the truth is he wish that we be in health; the truth is that during his earthly ministry, he was always moved with compassion and healing ALL! What more, he has not changed! -*"How God anointed Jesus of Nazareth with the Holy Ghost and with power: who went about doing good, and healing all that were oppressed of the devil; for God was with him." -Acts 10:38*. We can go on and on finding these truths in his word. Our part is to believe him for the manifestation of our healing regardless of the symptoms or how we feel, knowing he cannot lie, and cannot fail. So I invite you to *"... therefore come boldly unto the throne of grace, that we may obtain mercy, and find grace to help in time of need." -Hebrews 4:16*. It is well with you, in Jesus' name!

Anchor Scriptures:
Who his own self bare our sins in his own body on the tree, that we,

being dead to sins, should live unto righteousness: by whose stripes ye were healed. -1 Peter 2:24

He that commits sin is of the devil; for the devil sins from the beginning. For this purpose the Son of God was manifested, that he might destroy the works of the devil. - 1Jh 3:8

If the Son therefore shall make you free, you shall be free indeed. - John 8:36

Beloved, I wish above all things that thou mayest prosper and be in health, even as thy soul prospereth. -3 John 1:2

Worship the Lord your God, and his blessing will be on your food and water. I will take away sickness from among you -Exodus 23:25 (NIV)

Prayer:

In the name of Jesus, I am healed of any form of disease because the word of God confirms that he took all my sicknesses and diseases, and by His stripes I am healed. I declare today that I have total and complete healing. Every work of the devil in my spirit, soul and body is destroyed. Since the Lord has set me free, I am free indeed from every pain and discomfort. I live in divine health all the days of my life. God satisfies me with long life, and I live to, and enjoy, a good old age.

I thank you for your promise to me and stand on your word. I declare that henceforth, because I worship and serve you, my water and my food are blessed. No disease associated with food or liquid intake shall come near me and my family. Sicknesses and diseases are taken away from me and my family, in Jesus' name.

Declaration of Faith:

❖ *Wherefore God also hath highly exalted him, and given him a name which is above every name: That at the name of*

> *Jesus every knee should bow, of things in heaven, and things in earth, and things under the earth; -Philippians 2:9-10*

Father I speak to every sickness, I call you by name (mention its name) and command you to bow to the name of Jesus. In the name of Jesus, I cast you out of my body and declare that I am free of you, in Jesus' name.

> ❖ *Then they cried to the Lord in their trouble, and he saved them from their distress. He sent out his word and healed them; he rescued them from the grave. -Psalm 107:19, 20 (NIV)*

In the name of Jesus, The Lord hears my cry and delivers me from distresses and pains. His word heals me and I am rescued from the grave.

> ❖ *Heal me, Lord, and I will be healed; save me and I will be saved, for you are the one I praise. -Jeremiah 17:14 (NIV)*

> ❖ *I shall not die, but live, and declare the works of the Lord. -Psalms 118:17*

> ❖ *For I will restore health unto thee, and I will heal thee of thy wounds, saith the Lord; because they called thee an Outcast, saying, This is Zion, whom no man seeketh after. -Jeremiah 30:17*

Lord, I believe. I receive restoration of my health, and everything I have lost as a result of health problems, in Jesus' name.

I speak to every wound, be healed, in Jesus' name. I speak to every pain, be gone in Jesus' name! I speak to my bones, my blood, my flesh and every organ of my body, hear ye the word of the Lord - be healed, be made whole, in the name of Jesus!

> ❖ *As it is written: "I have made you a father of many nations." He is our father in the sight of God, in whom he believed— the God who gives life to the dead and calls into being things*

that were not. -Romans 4:17 (NIV)

I command every good thing that is dead in my body to come alive now, in the name of Jesus. By the resurrection power that raised Jesus from the dead, I declare that my organs are alive and function excellently. In the name of Jesus, everything that is missing in me is restored back. I live a healthy and fulfilled life.

Additional Scriptures:
Psalm 30:2; Exodus 15:26; Mark 5:34; James 5:16; Ps 107:19-20; Matthew 9:35; Psalm 34:6

Action Tips:
- Praise God for your healing; praise is your expression of faith that you believe he has healed you.
- Take specific scriptures impressed on your heart for this situation, and pray those at least daily (possibly more than once a day). Pray with these like you would take prescription drugs, because these are your "scripture prescriptions".
- Avoid negativity. Speak faith-filled words only.
- Avoid constantly reporting the symptoms, rather report what you believe God for ..."let the weak say I am strong" -Joel 3:10.
- Call those things that be not as though they were (Romans 4:17). Visualize yourself healed by God.

~~20~~
SCRIPTURE WORKS FOR HELP

For the Lord GOD will help me; therefore shall I not be confounded: therefore have I set my face like a flint, and I know that I shall not be ashamed. -Isaiah 50:7

God is our Help. When we look to him alone, confident that he is faithful to keep his promises to help us, he will move on our behalf; even in ways we never imagined possible. Let us come boldly, and ask for his help. He has promised that when we ask, we will receive (Matthew 7:7). He never pulls back from his promises to us (Numbers 23:19). Men may fail us, our God will never fail. He will never leave nor forsake you! (Deuteronomy 31:6)

Anchor Scriptures:
God is our refuge and strength, a very present help in trouble. - Psalms 46:1

The LORD is near to all who call on him, to all who call on him in truth. - Psalm 145:18

The LORD shall fight for you, and ye shall hold your peace. Exodus 14:14

For I the LORD thy God will hold thy right hand, saying unto thee, Fear not; I will help thee. -Isaiah 41:13

Fear thou not; for I am with thee: be not dismayed; for I am thy

God: I will strengthen thee; yea, I will help thee; yea, I will uphold thee with the right hand of my righteousness. -Isaiah 41:10

The righteous cry, and the LORD heareth, and delivereth them out of all their troubles. The LORD is nigh unto them that are of a broken heart; and saveth such as be of a contrite spirit. Many are the afflictions of the righteous: but the LORD delivereth him out of them all. -Psalms 34:17-19

Peace I leave with you; my peace I give you. I do not give to you as the world gives. Do not let your hearts be troubled and do not be afraid. -John 14:27 (NIV)

Prayer:
Father, in the name of Jesus, I thank you that you are my very present help in trouble. You word says we have not because we ask not, and so Father I come to you today, in the name of Jesus, asking for your help in this situation (**specifically mention where you need help right now**). I am not double minded, but rather I believe your word and I thank you for you are near to me, as I call upon you in faith. I thank you because you are holding my right hand, helping me and fighting all my battles. I declare today that God has strengthened me, and I have no more fear, in the name of Jesus. I am delivered out of all troubles and afflictions, in the name of Jesus! I receive the peace of God and my heart is no longer troubled, in Jesus' name. Father, I thank you and praise your holy name!

Declaration of Faith:
❖ *Give us help from trouble: for vain is the help of man. -Psalm 108:12*

Lord, I receive your help today, and I do not rely on any man. I believe that you will come through for me, in Jesus' name.

❖ *He that spared not his own Son, but delivered him up for us*

all, how shall he not with him also freely give us all things?
-Romans 8:32

Father, because you already gave me your son Jesus Christ, I know with him you will freely give me all other things. I thank you for helping me, and for the manifestation of my miracles.

❖ *Fear not, thou worm Jacob, and ye men of Israel; I will help thee, saith the LORD, and thy redeemer, the Holy One of Israel. - Isaiah 41:14*

My God is my Deliverer and my Helper. I receive his supernatural intervention in my situation today in Jesus' name.

And we know that all things work together for good to them that love God, to them who are the called according to his purpose. -Romans 8:28

I decree that all things begin to work for my good, because I love the Lord.

Additional Scriptures:
Psalm 121; Philippians 4:6-7; Psalm 27:9; 1Samuel 2:9; Psalm 34:7; Psalm 72:12

~~21~~
SCRIPTURE WORKS FOR HUSBANDS
(Praying God's Word over Your Wife)

In the same way, you husbands must give honor to your wives. Treat your wife with understanding as you live together. She may be weaker than you are, but she is your equal partner in God's gift of new life. Treat her as you should so your prayers will not be hindered. 1 Peter 3:7 (NLT)

When a man prays consistently for his wife, he not only blesses her life, but releases the power of God in his home to create an atmosphere of peace and order. God's word will fix anything and anyone, including you. If you have any troubling issues, as you pray God's word, he will move into your home, and set things right to the glory of his name. As the head of your home, when you stand in your place of authority and decree biblical blessings over your wife and home, it will come to pass. There will be increased love, peace and affection; and a sound foundation for your children's future.

Anchor Scriptures:

Whoso findeth a wife findeth a good thing, and obtaineth favour of the Lord. -Proverbs 18:22

Proverbs 31:10-31

A wise woman builds her home, but a foolish woman tears it down with her own hands. Proverbs 14:1 (NLT)

So ought men to love their wives as their own bodies. He that loveth his wife loveth himself. -Ephesians 5:28

Likewise, ye husbands, dwell with them according to knowledge, giving honour unto the wife, as unto the weaker vessel, and as being heirs together of the grace of life; that your prayers be not hindered. -1 Peter 3:7

But if any provide not for his own, and specially for those of his own house, he hath denied the faith, and is worse than an infidel. -1 Timothy 5:8

Prayer:
Father, I thank you for helping me find my wife (insert name). In agreement with your word, I have found a good wife; and I obtain favor from you Lord, in Jesus' name.

And so I confess and declare today that my wife is a virtuous woman. Her worth is far above rubies. She will do me good, and not evil, all the days of her life. She is smart, intelligent, the brightest and the best. She is submissive to God and to me, her husband. My wife is hardworking and not slothful. She is capable, and decisive. She lives in divine health and is able to meet her daily obligations without stress or toil. She is a strong person and respected by all around her. She is not afraid of tomorrow; her confidence is in God, so she looks at the future confidently. She speaks with wisdom, is loving and kind, and teaches others the same. Her children love and bless her. I, her husband, love her continually. She is a wise woman and builds her home. My wife is full of energy, and enjoys life, in the name of Jesus.

Father, as her husband, I love her as my own body, and as Christ loves the church. I dwell with her according to knowledge. I honor my wife, and together as joint heirs in Christ, we honor the Lord in our home. I thank you Lord, that my prayers will not be hindered. Today, I declare open doors over my life and I am able to always and continually provide for my household, in Jesus' name.

Declaration of Faith:

> ❖ *For the husband is the head of the wife, even as Christ is the head of the church: and he is the saviour of the body. – Ephesians 5:23*

I am a capable head of my family, even as Christ is the head of the church. I lead my family in love and with the wisdom of God.

Additional Scriptures:

Ephesians 5:24, 33; Colossians 3:19; Genesis 2:24; Proverbs 5:18-19; Proverbs 19:14

~~22~~
SCRIPTURE WORKS FOR JOY

A merry heart doeth good like a medicine: but a broken spirit drieth the bones. -Proverbs 17:22

You can have unspeakable joy in your life. Whenever you feel dry and depleted of joy, examine what you have been focusing on. When we focus more on what we think is going wrong around us, and not on the word of God, it depletes our energy. Get into the word of God for refreshing, and for the restoration of your joy. In his word we will find assurance. The Holy Spirit too is always ready to flood our hearts with joy when we ask him to. Let us ask now.

Anchor Scriptures:
For ye shall go out with joy, and be led forth with peace: the mountains and the hills shall break forth before you into singing, and all the trees of the field shall clap their hands. -Isaiah 55:12

For his anger endureth but a moment; in his favour is life: weeping may endure for a night, but joy cometh in the morning. -Psalms 30:5

Rejoice in the Lord alway: and again I say, Rejoice. -Philippians 4:4

And Nehemiah continued, "Go and celebrate with a feast of choice foods and sweet drinks, and share gifts of food with people who have nothing prepared. This is a sacred day before our Lord. Don't be dejected and sad, for the joy of the LORD is your strength!" -Nehemiah 8:10 (NLT)

This is the day which the LORD hath made; we will rejoice and be glad in it -Psalm 118:24

Be joyful in hope, patient in affliction, faithful in prayer. -Romans 12:12 (NIV)

There is a river whose streams make glad the city of God, the holy place where the Most High dwells. Psalm 46:4 (NIV)

Prayer:
Father, in the name of Jesus, I believe and declare today that the joy of the Lord is my strength. I go out with joy; I am led forth with peace. The mountains and the hills shall break forth before me into singing, and all the trees of the field shall clap their hands in celebration of me. All weeping ends in my life and I receive my joy now, in the name of Jesus. I rejoice always, and have no cause for sorrow. This is the day of my rejoicing. This is the day the Lord has made, and I will rejoice and be glad in it. The Most High God dwell in me, and the river of joy flows freely within me, in the mighty name of Jesus.

Declaration of Faith:
> ❖ *He will once again fill your mouth with laughter and your lips with shouts of joy. -Job 8:21 (NLT)*

My mouth is filled with laughter and rejoicing, every day of my life.

> ❖ *These things have I spoken unto you, that my joy might remain in you, and that your joy might be full. -John 15:11*

As I dwell on your word, I confess that the joy of the Lord remain and abide in me; and my joy is full. I will always rejoice and have reasons to celebrate God in my life.

> ❖ *Whom having not seen, ye love; in whom, though now ye see him not, yet believing, ye rejoice with joy unspeakable and full of glory: 1 Peter 1:8*

Lord, I believe in you and I experience joy unspeakable. My life radiates your glory, in Jesus name.

❖ *You have given me greater joy than those who have abundant harvests of grain and new wine. -Psalm 4:7 (NLT)*
Thank you Lord for giving greater joy!

May the God of hope fill me with all joy and peace as I trust in him, so that I will overflow with hope by the power of the Holy Spirit. –from Romans 15:13 (NIV)

Additional Scriptures:
Acts 2:28; Isaiah 12:3; John 7:38

Action Tips:
- ➤ To get your joy back spend time in the word of God like never before.
- ➤ Spend time in God's presence worshipping him.
- ➤ Focus on the testimonies and praise reports of what God did for you and others you know, or that you heard of, in the past.
- ➤ Be unwavering in your trust in God.
- ➤ Set an atmosphere of joy. If there is a special song that often lifts your spirit, play it, sing it, dance to it. Whatever lifts your spirit, as you pray these scriptures, engage in it.

May the Lord restore your Joy!

~~23~~
SCRIPTURE WORKS FOR LONGEVITY

With long life will I satisfy him, and shew him my salvation. - Psalms 91:16

God does not want your life cut short. His promise to us is for a long satisfied life. He wants us to fulfill his plans and purposes for us. As long as we dwell in his secret place, love and keep his commandments, we are guaranteed his protection, and a long life (Psalm 91).

Expect to live long. Believe God's word on protection; expect him to keep you and deliver you from all harm, sickness and diseases. Do not entertain any fear regarding your life, but believe the promise of God on living long, healthy and satisfied! Meditate his word on longevity, and this will boost your faith and confidence. You will "know" without any doubt that long life belongs to you!

Anchor Scriptures:
"No more babies dying in the cradle, or old people who don't enjoy a full lifetime; One-hundredth birthdays will be considered normal—anything less will seem like a cheat.

They'll build houses and move in. They'll plant fields and eat what they grow.

No more building a house that some outsider takes over, No more planting fields that some enemy confiscates, For my people will be as long-lived as trees, my chosen ones will have satisfaction in their work.

They won't work and have nothing come of it, they won't have children snatched out from under them. For they themselves are plantings blessed by God, with their children and grandchildren likewise God-

blessed.

Before they call out, I'll answer. Before they've finished speaking, I'll have heard..." says God.-Isaiah 65:20 - 24 (MSG)

He blesseth them also, so that they are multiplied greatly; and suffereth not their cattle to decrease -Psalm 107:38

And Moses was an hundred and twenty years old when he died: his eye was not dim, nor his natural force abated. —Deuteronomy 34:7

And such as do wickedly against the covenant shall he corrupt by flatteries: but the people that do know their God shall be strong, and do exploits. -Daniel 11:32

Prayer:

Father, I thank you for your word and I key into your promise to us your children. Your word says you satisfy us with long life, so today I receive long live spent in divine health and pleasure. Thank you because there shall be no death of any young person in my family and lineage. You are satisfying me with a good old age, as you have promised in your word. My eyes shall not grow dim, and my strength shall not fail as I gracefully grow older. A hundred years old shall be common place in my lineage, in the name of Jesus. All my life I shall not labor in vain, and I will enjoy the fruits of my labor. I am blessed and I multiply greatly. Because I know my God, I am strong and do exploits, in the name of Jesus.

Declaration of Faith:

❖ *And thou shalt go to thy fathers in peace; thou shalt be buried in a good old age. —Genesis 15:15*

I stand on your word, Lord. In the name of Jesus I will not die young. I will live long, and enjoy your peace and blessings all my life. I will leave this earth satisfied and fulfilled, in the name of Jesus.

❖ *Now Abraham was old, advanced in age; and the LORD*

had blessed Abraham in every way. Genesis 24:1

Like Abraham was old and advanced in age, so also will my testimony be. And the Lord will bless me in all things like he blessed Abraham. My life will be a blessing to many too, in Jesus' name.

<u>Additional Scriptures:</u>

Exodus 20:12; 2 Timothy 4:7; Judges 8:32; 1 Chronicles 29:28; Job 42:17

<u>Action Tips:</u>
- Believe God for long life, and see yourself live long.
- Set long term goals for yourself. Don't be afraid to do so.
- Take care of yourself and your health – eat right, exercise appropriately. Do all things in moderation.
- Forgive easily and don't hold grudges or bitterness in your heart.
- Get adequate rest.
- Enjoy the life God has given you, and be thankful.

~~24~~
SCRIPTURE WORKS FOR LOVE

But anyone who does not love does not know God, for God is love. - 1 John 4:8 (NLT)

Because God is love, it is only natural that he wants us to love too. But sometimes loving may seem difficult or almost impossible, but God has made provision for that in his word. When we make his word our final authority, and set ourselves to be obedient to him, regardless of our feelings, he will empower us to love as he loves. As you spend quality time in God's word, he will transform your heart. He will replace stony hearts with hearts of flesh (Ezekiel 36:26). He will fill you with his love.

If he asks us to love, it means we are capable of loving, regardless of who we have to deal with. Choose to love. Yes, make a decision to love! Invite the Holy Spirit to fill your heart with the love of God. Love by faith, and show it by your works. Refuse to be discouraged by the people you have to deal with. Love never fails! (1 Corinthians 13:8)

Anchor Scriptures:
Don't just pretend to love others. Really love them. Hate what is wrong. Hold tightly to what is good. - Romans 12:9 (NLT)

And hope maketh not ashamed; because the love of God is shed abroad in our hearts by the Holy Ghost which is given unto us. - Romans 5:5

He answered: "'Love the Lord your God with all your heart and with all your soul and with all your strength and with all your mind'; and, 'Love your neighbor as yourself.'" -Luke 10:27 (NIV)

Love is patient, love is kind. It does not envy, it does not boast, it is not proud. It does not dishonor others, it is not self-seeking, it is not easily angered, it keeps no record of wrongs. Love does not delight in evil but rejoices with the truth. It always protects, always trusts, always hopes, always perseveres. Love never fails. But where there are prophecies, they will cease; where there are tongues, they will be stilled; where there is knowledge, it will pass away. -1 Corinthians 13:4-8

Prayer:

In the name of Jesus, I am not pretentious. I sincerely love people, and care for them. I hate what is wrong, and hold tightly to what is good. The love of God is shed abroad in my heart by the Holy Spirit who dwells within me. I love the Lord my God with my whole heart, soul and mind; and I love my neighbor as myself. I love as God loves. I confess today that I am patient, I am kind. I do not envy, I do not boast, I am not proud. I don't dishonor others, I am not self-seeking, I am not easily angered, and I keep no record of wrongs. I, (your name) do not delight in evil but rejoices with the truth. I always protect, always trust, always hope, and always persevere. God's love in me will never fail, in Jesus' name.

Declaration of Faith:

❖ *Do to others as you would have them do to you. -Luke 6:31(NIV)*

In the name of Jesus, I am good to people, and I treat others with love and respect, as I would want to be treated.

❖ *Love does no wrong to others, so love fulfills the requirements of God's law. -Romans 13:10 (NLT)*

I do no wrong to others. I will only be a source of blessings to all, in Jesus' name. I will fulfill God's law to love others, and be a shining light in this world.

Additional Scriptures:
Ephesians 4:2; Proverbs 10:12; 1 John 4:7, 18-19; 1 John 3:1; Proverbs 17:9

Action Tips:
- Love God. Seek after him. Spend time with God daily, in his word, in praise, in prayers and listening to messages about him.
- Love yourself. Don't belittle yourself, in your heart or before others; and don't think more highly of yourself than you ought to, as well.
- Love others, as God has commanded. Take time to do acts of love and kindness to those around you. Remember you are the sermon they "hear" when they meet you.
- Don't keep record of wrongs. Choose to forgive, even if it's not asked for.

~~25~~
SCRIPTURE WORKS FOR MARRIAGE

"So they are no longer two, but one flesh. What therefore God has joined together, let no man separate." -Matthew 19:6 (NASB)

Marriage is an institution ordained by God, because "it is not good for man to be alone" (Genesis 2:18). God instituted marriage for us to help one another on this earth; and also to raise godly seed/offspring (Malachi 2:15). We are to complement each other, not to be in competition. "A kingdom divided against itself cannot stand", Jesus said in Mark 3:24. Therefore, unity in the family is very important, not just for ourselves, but also for the children we raise in our families.

A marriage that is founded on, and continues in the word and love of God will not fail, regardless of what storms come against it. This is why it is important to invite God into our marriages, obeying his commands on marriage and making him Lord of our homes. God's word will guide you; it will instruct you on how to have a successful and harmonious marriage; and it will empower you to live successfully in your married life.

If you desire marriage, ask the Lord, reminding him of his promises on marriage, and he will answer you. He will give you the desires of your heart, if you delight in him, and truly seek to please him only (Psalm 37:4). If you need stability and unity in your home, ask the Lord for it too, based on his word. If your marriage is stable and a great example of a Christian marriage, praise God and cover your home from any attack of the evil one. You have victory in Jesus' name!

For the Single Seeking a Godly Spouse:
Anchor Scriptures:
God sets the solitary in families: he brings out those who are bound with chains: but the rebellious dwell in a dry land. -Psalm 68:6

And the LORD God said, It is not good that the man should be alone; I will make him a helper suitable for him. -Genesis 2:18

Whoso findeth a wife findeth a good thing, and obtaineth favour of the LORD. -Proverbs 18:22

Behold, I send an Angel before you, to keep you in the way, and to bring you into the place which I have prepared. -Exodus 23:20

For he is our peace, who hath made both one, and hath broken down the middle wall of partition between us; -Ephesians 2:14

Prayer:
Father, I thank you because your promises are true. I bless your name for the gift of life and for making me fit to be married. I ask, in the name of Jesus that I obtain favor from you Lord. Your word says it is not good for man to be alone, so I will not be alone. I am led of God, my steps are ordered of him; and his angels bring me in contact with my God-ordained spouse. I declare that I am married to the right person for me. God sets me in my own family, and I enjoy family live. Every chain holding me captive is broken, and every force stopping my marriage is destroyed by the power of God, in the name of Jesus.

I live a life of commitment and faithfulness. The Lord is pruning me and getting me ready to be married; as he brings me and my future spouse together. You are making us one. Every middle wall of partition between us is broken right now, in the name of Jesus! I believe I receive my marriage today, in the name of Jesus. I will not be confused or deceived. I will not bend God's rules, but will walk in chastity and purity.

Your word says your sheep hear your voice. In the name of Jesus, I hear your voice concerning who my future spouse is, the voice of the stranger I will not hear. I thank you for provision for my wedding, and for a glorious married life, in Jesus' name I have prayed.

Action Tips:
- As you pray, listen for instructions from God, and follow these instructions. Are there things you are doing that you need to stop? Or are there things you need to be doing that you are not? If you sincerely ask, he will show you.
- Give him thanks for answering your prayers, and enjoy this period of your life. Don't be anxious, and don't be worried. Those are expressions of a lack of faith.
- Relax, let go, and let God order your steps. Don't try working things out for yourself, trust God. Only he knows the heart of every being.
- Devote time to the service of God.
- Use this time of waiting to develop a strong relationship with God.
- Truly seek God!

For the Married Couple:
Anchor Scriptures:
Thy kingdom come. Thy will be done in earth, as it is in heaven. – Matthew 6:10

Again I say unto you, That if two of you shall agree on earth as touching any thing that they shall ask, it shall be done for them of my Father which is in heaven. -Matthew 18:19

Prayer:
Father in the name of Jesus, let your kingdom be

established in our home, and let only your will be done in our family. Lord Jesus, we enthrone you Lord over our home, and dethrone every false gods in our lives. We declare from this day that there is unity in our home, and as we agree and pray on any issue, as a family, we see results. God is moving on our behalf. In the name of Jesus, no person and nothing shall put what God has joined together asunder. We nullify every plan of the enemy against our home. We shall never be divided. We stand strong together as the army of the Most High God. We produce godly offspring in this home and are faithful to one another. We destroy every ungodly influence on our marriage and cover this marriage with the blood of Jesus.

Additional Scriptures:
2 Corinthians 6:14; Hebrews 13:4; Mark 10:6-9; Malachi 2:15

Action Tips:
- Next to God, make your spouse and family a priority.
- Respect and honor one another.
- Make time for your family.
- Spend quality time together, no matter how busy your schedules, find a time that works for all.
- Pray together daily; and pray for one another in your personal prayer times.
- Share the day's experiences together. Talk; laugh together, just like you did in courtship. Rekindle your love for each other daily.
- Express your love for each other.

~~26~~
SCRIPTURE WORKS FOR OVERCOMING CONDEMNATION

There is therefore now no condemnation to them which are in Christ Jesus, who walk not after the flesh, but after the Spirit. –Romans 8:1

Condemnation is one of the enemy's greatest tactics to get a Christian feeling defeated, and incapable. And like every other trick of the devil, it is nothing but another lie! God has promised to lift us back up when we fall. But for many believers, even after the Lord lifts them back up, their minds are still down there in the mess. If the Lord has forgiven, and forgotten it, why keep replaying it in your mind? If the Lord let it go, why do you still hold on to it? God has forgiven you, why not forgive yourself?

We have an Advocate in our Lord Jesus Christ, and he has given us power to overcome all the wiles of the enemy. Wake up! Grab your sword of the Spirit (the word of God) Ephesians 6:17. Take a stand against the accuser of the brethren, the devil, and take your rightful place in the Lord – You are righteous through Christ; you are a saint, forgiven, glorified, loved of God, a mighty warrior, a disciple of Christ, beloved of God, special to God. Don't be cheated by the devil one more day! *"So if the Son sets you free, you are truly free."* –John 8:36 (NLT)

Anchor Scriptures:
Casting down imaginations, and every high thing that exalteth itself against the knowledge of God, and bringing into captivity every thought

to the obedience of Christ; -2 Corinthians 10:5

Put on the whole armour of God, that ye may be able to stand against the wiles of the devil. -Ephesians 6:12

Finally, brethren, whatsoever things are true, whatsoever things are honest, whatsoever things are just, whatsoever things are pure, whatsoever things are lovely, whatsoever things are of good report; if there be any virtue, and if there be any praise, think on these things. -Philippians 4:8

There is therefore now no condemnation to them which are in Christ Jesus, who walk not after the flesh, but after the Spirit. For the law of the Spirit of life in Christ Jesus hath made me free from the law of sin and death. -Romans 8:1-2

Prayer:

In the name of Jesus, I bring all my thoughts captive under the obedience of Christ. I cast down every imagination, and every high thing exalting itself against the knowledge of the truth of God's word in my life. I put on the whole armor of God, and overcome every lie and trick of the enemy. My mind is sanctified by the blood of Jesus. I think of only things that are true according to the word of God; and that truth says I am redeemed by the blood of Jesus. I think only of things that are praise-worthy, that are lovely and of good report.

You foul spirit of condemnation; I command you out of my mind, my spirit, my soul, my thoughts, and my body, in the name of Jesus - For the law of the Spirit of life in Christ Jesus has made me free from the law of sin and death. I receive the joy of the Lord. I have divine peace. I know my God and I do spiritual exploits to the glory of his name. In Jesus' name!

Declaration of Faith:

❖ *If we confess our sins, he is faithful and just to forgive us our sins, and to cleanse us from all unrighteousness. -1 John 1:9*

I have confessed my sins. I am forgiven and cleansed from all unrighteousness. I receive God's forgiveness in the name of Jesus.

> ❖ *This is the covenant that I will make with them after those days, saith the Lord, I will put my laws into their hearts, and in their minds will I write them; And their sins and iniquities will I remember no more. -Hebrews 10:16-17*

I remember my sins no more, just as God remembers them no more. His laws are in my heart, and written in my mind, so my life will always please the Lord, my God.

Additional Scriptures:
John 3:17; Romans 8:34; John 8:11

~~27~~
SCRIPTURE WORKS FOR OVERCOMING DEPRESSION

My flesh and my heart may fail, but God is the strength of my heart and my portion forever. -Psalms 73:26 (NIV)

Depression is defined in the Merriam Webster dictionary as "a state of feeling sad". It is also defined as "a serious medical condition in which the person feels very sad, hopeless, and unimportant…" Regardless of its definitions, the word God is powerful and able to destroy the yoke of depression on your life!

Depression is devil's weapon for keeping us away from the presence of God, thereby causing more harm. *"A merry heart doeth good like a medicine: but a broken spirit drieth the bones." (Proverbs 17:22)*. David in the bible expressed his depression so many times in the Psalms. But he always turned to God, and was an ardent worshipper of God, and God delivered him. God wants us to *"Rejoice in the Lord always, and again I say, Rejoice" -Philippians 4:4*. The ERV puts it this way: *"Always be filled with joy in the Lord. I will say it again. Be filled with joy"*. Receive the oil of gladness, and be spurred into endless joy, in Jesus' name (Isaiah 61:3).

Bring God's presence into your situation; turn on your praise. Openly declare his word of freedom and liberty over your life. Worship him, and the spirit of depression must flee! Give him a sacrifice of praise, praising even when you don't feel like. May you be delivered from the spirit of depression, in Jesus' name.

Anchor Scriptures:
Why are you downcast, O my soul? Why so disturbed within me? Put your hope in God, for I will yet praise him, my Savior and my God. -Psalms 42:5 (NIV)

A cheerful heart is good medicine, but a crushed spirit dries up the bones. -Proverbs 17:22 (NIV)

For I know the thoughts that I think toward you, saith the LORD, thoughts of peace, and not of evil, to give you an expected end. -Jeremiah 29:11

Finally, brethren, whatsoever things are true, whatsoever things are honest, whatsoever things are just, whatsoever things are pure, whatsoever things are lovely, whatsoever things are of good report; if there be any virtue, and if there be any praise, think on these things. -Philippians 4:8

Then he said unto them, Go your way, eat the fat, and drink the sweet, and send portions unto them for whom nothing is prepared: for this day is holy unto our Lord: neither be ye sorry; for the joy of the Lord is your strength. Nehemiah 8:10

And I will ask the Father, and He will give you another Comforter (Counselor, Helper, Intercessor, Advocate, Strengthener, and Standby), that He may remain with you forever -John 14:16 (AMP)

These things have I spoken unto you, that my joy might remain in you, and that your joy might be full. -John 15:11

Prayer:
In the name of Jesus, I have the joy of the Lord. I rejoice always. Out of my belly shall flow rivers of living waters. I have the peace of God that passes all understanding. I speak to my soul now; hope in God. My heart is merry and so my health is perfect, in the name of Jesus. I think and focus only on things that are good, pure, lovely, praise worthy and of

good report. I know and believe that the plans of God for me are of good, to give me hope and a future, so I rejoice in the Lord and I am strengthened in my inner man, in Jesus' name.

Holy Spirit, my Comforter, my dependable Helper, my Intercessor, my Strengthener, my Advocate, I invite you into my life afresh. I begin to experience your love as you comfort and help me come out of any and all forms of depression. I declare that I have an understanding of your love for me. Your joy remains in me, and my joy is full. Thank you Lord, for I am delivered from the spirit of depression. Depression is a thing of the past and gone forever from my life in the name of Jesus.

Declaration of Faith:

❖ *Know ye not that ye are the temple of God, and that the Spirit of God dwelleth in you? -1 Corinthians 3:16*

Holy Spirit, I receive you into my life anew. Because the Spirit of God dwells in me, therefore depression cannot dwell in me anymore. I am free in Jesus' name.

❖ *Though you have not seen him, you love him; and even though you do not see him now, you believe in him and are filled with an inexpressible and glorious joy, -1 Peter 1:8 (NIV)*

I receive joy unspeakable and inexpressible in my spirit today, in Jesus' name.

❖ *Casting down imaginations, and every high thing that exalteth itself against the knowledge of God, and bringing into captivity every thought to the obedience of Christ; -2 Corinthians 10:5*

In the name of Jesus, I cast down every imagination and argument of the mind that is against the knowledge of God in me. I bring all my thoughts captive, and command them to be obedient to Christ.

Additional Scriptures:

Psalm 40:1-3; Psalm 32:10; Deuteronomy 31:8;

Corinthians 1:3-4

Action points:
- Saturate your environment with faith-filled music.
- Praise and worship God more.
- Rest, exercise and eat well. If possible create a time when you stop everything and just rest, sleep or just relax listening to the word of God.
- Flush out negativity from your mind. Confess God's word over and over.
- Focus your mind on things that bring you joy and gladdens your heart.

~~28~~
SCRIPTURE WORKS FOR OVERCOMING FEAR

There is no fear in love; but perfect love casteth out fear: because fear hath torment. He that feareth is not made perfect in love. -1 John 4:18

Fear has torment! You are too protected by God to be tormented! He has made every provision for us to be free from fear; and he constantly tells us in the bible to "Fear Not". In fact "Fear Not" is said to appear in the bible 365 times! There you go, you have one for every day!

FEAR NOT! You have God's word that is sharper than any two-edged sword (Hebrews 4:12). You have the Blood of Jesus that speaks better things than the blood of Abel (Hebrews 12:24), speaking for you and on your behalf. You also have the Holy Spirit of God, the power of the Most High that no demonic power can withstand. You have authority in the Name of Jesus, and at his name every knee MUST bow! (Philippians 2:10). And you have the Angels waiting on you, hearkening unto the voice of God's word! There is nothing to fear. Cast out that evil spirit of fear, in the name of Jesus! Receive boldness and a sound mind, in Jesus' name.

Anchor Scriptures:

For God has not given us the spirit of fear; but of power, and of love, and of a sound mind. -2 Timothy 1:7

He shall not be afraid of evil tidings: his heart is fixed, trusting in the LORD. -Psalm 112:7

Fear not; for I am with you: be not dismayed; for I am your God: I will strengthen you; yea, I will help you; yea, I will uphold you with the right hand of my righteousness. -Isaiah 41:10

The wicked flee when no man pursueth: but the righteous are bold as a lion. -Proverbs 28:1

The angel of the LORD encamps around those who fear Him, And rescues them. -Psalm 34:7

The LORD is my light and my salvation; whom shall I fear? the LORD is the strength of my life; of whom shall I be afraid?
When the wicked, even mine enemies and my foes, came upon me to eat up my flesh, they stumbled and fell. -Psalm 27:1-2

Prayer:
In the name of Jesus, I come against the spirit of fear. I receive the Spirit of God, and I have power, love and a sound mind. I will not be afraid of evil tidings: my heart is fixed, trusting in the Lord. I am free of fear, and I'm not dismayed. My God is strengthening me, he gives me power and he upholds me with the right hand of his righteousness. Through faith in Jesus Christ, I am righteous; and I am as bold as a lion. I fear nothing and no one. The angels of the Lord encamp round about me. Because I fear and serve God, no evil can touch me. The Lord is my light and my salvation; whom shall I fear? The Lord is the strength of my life; of whom shall I be afraid? The wicked that rise up against me and my destiny shall stumble and fall for my sake, in Jesus' name.

Declaration of Faith:
❖ *Fear not [there is nothing to fear] -Isaiah 41:10 (AMP)*
In the name of Jesus, there is nothing to fear in my life, so I will fear not.

❖ *For I am the LORD, your God, who takes hold of your right hand and says to you, Do not fear; I will help you. - Isaiah 41:13 (NIV)*

Lord, I thank you for your promise to help me. I receive your help today, and all fear is gone, in the name of Jesus.

❖ *And Moses said unto the people, Fear ye not, stand still, and see the salvation of the LORD, which he will shew to you to day: for the Egyptians whom ye have seen to day, ye shall see them again no more for ever. - Exodus 14:13*

In the name of Jesus, I stand firm in faith trusting you for my deliverance and salvation. Every source of fear in my life today disappears and I see them no more in the name of Jesus. Father, I ask you to take over, and I take your peace in place of my fears.

Additional Scriptures:
Philippians 4:6; Psalms 56:3; Romans 8:14-15; Psalms 34:4; Jeremiah 20:11

Action Tips:
- Build up your knowledge of the word of God. Spend time daily reading and meditating the bible.
- Jot down verses that admonish you to not be afraid.
- Confess and believe the word. Speak it to yourself.
- Walk in love. Perfect love cast out fear -1 John 4:18.
- Love the Lord; love people. Ask the Holy Spirit to help you.

~~29~~
SCRIPTURE WORKS FOR OVERCOMING GRIEF & SORROW

And God shall wipe away all tears from their eyes; and there shall be no more death, neither sorrow, nor crying, neither shall there be any more pain: for the former things are passed away. -Revelation 21:4

If you have suffered a loss, or going through a period of sorrow, know that the Lord is right there with you. He has promised never to leave nor forsake you (Deuteronomy 31:8). We do not have a High Priest that is not moved by our feelings (Hebrews 4:15). He will comfort you. Don't withdraw from God, let this be your most intimate time with him, and he will see you through; and heal your heart.

Make his word your companion. He will speak his love to your heart through his word. He will give you his peace as you fix your eyes on him through meditating and praying the word of God.

Anchor Scriptures:

And we know that all things work together for good to them that love God, to them who are the called according to his purpose. - Romans 8:28

Thou hast caused men to ride over our heads; we went through fire and through water: but thou broughtest us out into a wealthy place. - Psalms 66:12

I will not leave you comfortless: I will come to you. -John 14:18

Blessed are they that mourn: for they shall be comforted. —Matthew 5:4

The LORD is nigh unto them that are of a broken heart; and saveth such as be of a contrite spirit. -Psalm 34:18

For his anger endureth but a moment; in his favour is life: weeping may endure for a night, but joy cometh in the morning. —Psalm 30:5

The eternal God is thy refuge, and underneath are the everlasting arms: and he shall thrust out the enemy from before thee; and shall say, Destroy them. —Deuteronomy 33:27

Prayer:

Lord, I thank you for all your promises to me. I pray that all things work together for my good, regardless of my current state. I receive your strength, and I know you are bringing me out with joy and gladness. Lord, help me feel your embrace. Touch my heart today. Let me feel your presence like never before. Hold me in your everlasting arms. May I be comforted, in the name of Jesus. I thank you because my mourning and sorrow ends, and my joy come in Jesus' name.

Declaration of Faith:

❖ *When you pass through the waters, I will be with you; and when you pass through the rivers, they will not sweep over you. When you walk through the fire, you will not be burned; the flames will not set you ablaze.* -Isaiah 43:2 (NIV)

I thank you Lord, for your word. Thank you for helping me through this; and for being with me every step of the way. I will make it through this period, and come out triumphant, in Jesus' name.

❖ *Yea, though I walk through the valley of the shadow of death,*

I will fear no evil: for thou art with me; thy rod and thy staff they comfort me. -Psalm 23:4

I receive your comfort today, O Lord. I fear no evil. I trust you with my future, Lord. I receive the strength to keep on.

Additional Scriptures:

Romans 8:38; Psalm 119:50; Isaiah 40:31; 2 Corinthians 12:9; Psalm 73:26; Deuteronomy 31:6

Action Tips:

- Commune with God, and read the word more than ever.
- It is okay to cry, let it out if you need to.
- Don't isolate yourself. Receive the love of those around you.
- Receive help when people offer it.
- Give help to others. Serve where needed, or volunteer if you can.
- Be busy. Try not to be alone all the time during the initial stage of this test. Go out, if you can; take a walk, visit the library…find a way to be occupied.
- Saturate your environment with music of praise and worship.

~~30~~
SCRIPTURE WORKS FOR PEACE

You will keep in perfect peace all who trust in you, all whose thoughts are fixed on you! -Isaiah 26:3 (NLT)

There is nothing that can be compared to the peace of God. It stabilizes us; it calms us in the midst of turmoil. It brings us rest when everything around us is in chaos. The peace of God is beyond human comprehension. It's the reason people will think you're weird when challenges don't break you down. It is the same reason many will be drawn to you, to know the source of your peace – God. The peace of God is the presence of an unshakable faith and trust in the Lord; and because faith will bring you desired results, this peace will keep you from making wrong choices and decisions while you wait on the Lord. This peace from God is available if you ask for it… *"Ask and it shall be given you"* - Matthew 7:7

Anchor Scriptures:
Peace I leave with you, my peace I give unto you: not as the world giveth, give I unto you. Let not your heart be troubled, neither let it be afraid. -John 14:27

And the peace of God, which passeth all understanding, shall keep your hearts and minds through Christ Jesus. -Philippians 4:7

Great peace have those who love your law, and nothing can make them stumble. -Psalm 119:165(NIV)

Prayer:
In the name of Jesus, I receive the peace of God today. Father, you are the Prince of Peace, I ask for your total peace that passes all understanding. I pray that your peace keep my heart and mind. That my eyes and thoughts be fixed on you, trusting in you. And because I trust in you, I am kept in perfect peace. I am not moved by situations around me. I remain steadfast in my faith and confidence in you. Your peace surrounds me at all times, in Jesus' name. Nothing will move me Lord, because I love your law.

Declaration of Faith:
> ❖ *And I will give peace in the land, and ye shall lie down, and none shall make you afraid: and I will rid evil beasts out of the land, neither shall the sword go through your land - Leviticus 26:6*

I live in peace in this land. I lie down and wake up in the peace of God. I shall not be afraid. No evil shall come near me in any form; and I shall not die but live, in Jesus' name.

> ❖ *The LORD will give strength unto his people; the LORD will bless his people with peace -Psalm 29:11*

I am yours Lord, so I receive the blessing of the peace of God today, in Jesus' name.

> ❖ *Be careful for nothing; but in every thing by prayer and supplication with thanksgiving let your requests be made known unto God. And the peace of God, which passeth all understanding, shall keep your hearts and minds through Christ Jesus. - Philippians 4:6-7*

Lord, thank you that you have heard my prayers. I receive the peace of God concerning every issue in my life. I have your peace that passes the understanding of men.

Additional Scriptures:
Jeremiah 29:11; John 16:33; Isaiah 26:12; Ephesians 2:14

Action points:
- Meditate on the love of God through his word, the Bible.
- Choose to trust God, no matter what.
- Speak words of God's faithfulness to yourself often. Reassure yourself of his love for you.
- Hang around, and fellowship with other believers that exudes God's presence in their lives.
- Be purposefully thankful.

~~31~~
SCRIPTURE WORKS FOR PREGNANCY

Lo, children are an heritage of the LORD: and the fruit of the womb is his reward. - Psalm 127:3

Are you married and desire the fruit of the womb? Let your mind be at peace. God wants you fruitful, he wants you to multiply, and he will bless you with children. If you are expecting already, his hand will be over you and your baby, and bring you to a safe delivery. As you pray in faith with the bible verses below, the Lord will answer your prayers; regardless of medical reports, or your past experiences. God's word is powerful and creative! He will make you a joyful parent. Believe the report of the Lord.

Believing for the Fruit of the Womb:
There shall nothing cast their young, nor be barren, in thy land: the number of thy days I will fulfil. -Exodus 23:26

He gives the childless woman a family, making her a happy mother. Praise the LORD! -Psalm 113:9

Prayer:
Dear Lord, I thank you for your promises, and your faithfulness. I thank you that you are more than able to do what you have promised. Today, I come boldly unto your throne of grace, and ask, in the name of Jesus, that you make me a mother of children. Your word says we shall not be barren, so I speak to my womb today: O ye womb, hear the word of the Lord: in the name of Jesus, be open, be fruitful. I declare today that my womb will carry my children. Everything that is in me that has not been planted by the Lord is uprooted, in the name of Jesus. I speak life to my

womb. My womb, come alive, in Jesus' name. I speak to every reproductive organ in my body, be fruitful, and reproduce, according to God's original plan. I receive the reward of the fruit of the womb from the Lord today. Thank you Father, because I will carry my own children too, in the name of Jesus.

Praying for Safe Delivery:
Being confident of this very thing, that he which hath begun a good work in you will perform it until the day of Jesus Christ: -Philippians 1:6

I know that, whatsoever God doeth, it shall be for ever: nothing can be put to it, nor any thing taken from it: and God doeth it, that men should fear before him. -Ecclesiastes 3:14

Shall I bring to the birth, and not cause to bring forth? saith the LORD: shall I cause to bring forth, and shut the womb? saith thy God. -Isaiah 66:9

Prayer:
Father, I worship and adore you this day. I thank you for blessing me with the fruit of the womb. I thank you that you who have started a good work in me will complete it. I thank you because you have brought me this far, and you will be with me to the end of this journey, when I will carry my baby in my hands. I know that whatsoever you do is forever, and nothing can be done to change it, and so I declare today that no evil shall befall me and my baby. There shall not be any evil report concerning me and this pregnancy.

I thank you for perfect health during this period. I thank you for an enjoyable supernatural pregnancy and childbirth. I receive your strength all through, in Jesus' name. I declare that no weapon formed against me or my baby, or anyone in my family, shall prosper. As you are adding this baby to us, we shall know this time for good; and our lives shall be truly enriched. Thank you for divine provision; thank you that this baby and this family shall not lack, but rather we shall enjoy your abundance and love. Thank you for a safe delivery, and for the right medical help. I decree that only those that you have ordained to help with this delivery shall be present on the day of delivery. There will be no complications, in the name of Jesus. You will give all the medical staff attending to us your wisdom and your Holy Spirit will take over all that will be done on the day of the delivery. In Jesus' name I have prayed.

Declaration of Faith:
❖ *And God blessed them, and God said unto them, Be fruitful, and multiply, and replenish the earth, and subdue it: and have dominion over the fish of the sea, and over the fowl of the air, and over every living thing that moveth upon the earth. -Genesis 1:28*

I am fruitful; I multiply and replenish the earth. I have my own children, and fulfill God's command and purpose, in the name of Jesus.

❖ *And the midwives said unto Pharaoh, Because the Hebrew women are not as the Egyptian women; for they are lively, and are delivered ere the midwives come in unto them. -Exodus 1:19*

Lord, I have supernatural strength as I deliver my child. I thank you that even the medical personnel present will testify to your power in this delivery, and glorify your name. Thank you for a smooth and problem free delivery, in Jesus' name.

❖ *Thou shalt be blessed above all people: there shall not be male or female barren among you, or among your cattle. -Deuteronomy 7:14*

Hallelujah! Lord I exalt your name because I shall not be barren according to your word, in Jesus' name.

Additional Scriptures:
Psalm 128:3; Philippians 4:13; Psalm 84:11

~~32~~
SCRIPTURE WORKS FOR PROTECTION & SAFETY

Yea, though I walk through the valley of the shadow of death, I will fear no evil: for thou art with me; thy rod and thy staff they comfort me - Psalm 23:4

God will protect you, trust him! No one who trusts in him will be ashamed. He is the Almighty, he is the Man of War who has never lost a battle before; and never will. He has his angels encamping round about you (Psalm 34:7) to protect and deliver you. He never sleeps nor slumbers because he is keeping watch over you. Build up your faith in his ability to protect you by meditating scriptures on his protection and declaring these over yourself, and yours. Believe God's word.

Anchor Scripture:
Psalm 91

Prayer:
I dwell in the secret place of the Most High and abide under the shadow of the Almighty. I say of the LORD, he is my refuge and my fortress: my God; in him will I trust. Surely he shall deliver me from the snare of the fowler, and from the noisome pestilence. He shall cover me with his feathers, and under his wings shall I trust: his truth shall be my shield and buckler. I shall not be afraid for the terror by night; nor for the arrow that flies by day; Nor for the pestilence that walks in darkness; nor for the destruction that wastes at noonday. A thousand shall fall at my side, and ten thousand at my right

hand; but it shall not come nigh me. Only with my eyes shall I behold and see the reward of the wicked.

Because I have made the LORD, which is my refuge, even the most High, my habitation; there shall no evil befall me, neither shall any plague come near my dwelling. For he shall give his angels charge over me, to keep me in all my ways. They shall bear me up in their hands, lest I dash my foot against a stone. I shall tread upon the lion and adder: the young lion and the dragon shall I trample under feet. Because I have set my love upon God, therefore will he deliver me. He will set me on high, because I have known his name. I shall call upon him, and he will answer me: he will be with me in trouble; he (my God) will deliver me, and honor me. With long life will he satisfy me, and show me his salvation.

-Adapted from Psalms 91:1-16

Declaration of Faith:

> ❖ *For I will surely deliver thee, and thou shalt not fall by the sword, but thy life shall be for a prey unto thee: because thou hast put thy trust in me, saith the LORD - Jeremiah 39:18*

In Jesus' name, I am delivered; I will not be a victim of evil because I trust in my God.

> ❖ *Because he hath set his love upon me, therefore will I deliver him: I will set him on high, because he hath known my name. He shall call upon me, and I will answer him: I will be with him in trouble; I will deliver him, and honor him. - Psalm 91:14-15*

My God answers me when I call on him, because I know his name. He will deliver me from all plans of the evil one. He will be with me at all times and will honor me, in Jesus' name.

Additional Scriptures:

Psalm 121; Proverbs 30:5; Matthew 10:30-31

~~33~~
SCRIPTURE WORKS FOR PROVISION/DIVINE SUPPLY

Look at the birds. They don't plant or harvest or store food in barns, for your heavenly Father feeds them. And aren't you far more valuable to him than they are? -Matthew 6:26 (NLT)

The story of the widow with her last meal is just one of several testimonies of God's ability to supernaturally provide for his people (I Kings 17:8-16). We also read about God providing for the children of Israel in the wilderness (Isaiah 48:21). We read of him feeding thousands with just five loaves and two fishes (Mark 6:41). He is still supernaturally providing for his people today. Trust him as your Provider. Be consistent in giving your tithes and offerings. Give him your own "five loaves and two fishes", and watch him multiply it. You can never out-give God. He will reward your faithfulness and trust. He will supply all your needs! As you plant your seed through your giving, water it with the word of God. Pray his word on the rewards of giving; and be expectant of your harvest.

Anchor Scriptures:
You will have plenty to eat, until you are full, and you will praise the name of the LORD your God, who has worked wonders for you; never again will my people be shamed. -Joel 2:26 (NIV)

The Lord is my shepherd; I shall not want. - Psalm 23:1

Be glad then, ye children of Zion, and rejoice in the LORD your

God: for he hath given you the former rain moderately, and he will cause to come down for you the rain, the former rain, and the latter rain in the first month. And the floors shall be full of wheat, and the fats shall overflow with wine and oil. And I will restore to you the years that the locust hath eaten, the cankerworm, and the caterpiller, and the palmerworm, my great army which I sent among you. -Joel 2:23-25

And my God will meet all your needs according to the riches of his glory in Christ Jesus. - Philippians 4:19 (NIV)

He provides food for those who fear him; he remembers his covenant forever. -Psalm 111:5

The LORD shall open unto thee his good treasure, the heaven to give the rain unto thy land in his season, and to bless all the work of thine hand: and thou shalt lend unto many nations, and thou shalt not borrow. -Deuteronomy 28:12

Now he who supplies seed to the sower and bread for food will also supply and increase your store of seed and will enlarge the harvest of your righteousness. -2 Corinthians 9:10 (NIV)

Prayer:
Father, in the name of Jesus, I thank you for your assurance of provision. I thank you because you are my God, my Lord, my Shepherd, and my only Source. Therefore I know I will lack no good thing, in Jesus' name. You are the Lord that provides, and you assure us that when we ask we receive. Father, I ask for (mention your needs), and I thank you because I believe I receive your supernatural provision in the name of Jesus. I believe your word that you are meeting all of my needs, so I will not worry about anything.

In the name of Jesus, I have an abundance of supplies. As I give, you are causing people to give to me. Thank you for opening up the windows of heaven unto me, and pouring out your blessings on me. The Lord is opening up his good treasure to me. The showers of blessings are being released on my life. All the works of my hands are blessed. I shall not borrow but lend unto many, because I have more than enough, in Jesus' name. Thank you Lord for increase in my life. Thank you for my bountiful harvest, in agreement with your word. I thank you because you are faithful. I believe I receive my petition this day, in Jesus' name I pray.

Declaration of Faith:
> ❖ *But seek ye first the kingdom of God, and his righteousness; and all these things shall be added unto you.* -Matthew 6:33

As I continue to seek you Lord, the blessings of God are continually added unto me, in Jesus' name.

> ❖ *The young lions do lack, and suffer hunger: but they that seek the LORD shall not want any good thing.* -Psalm 34:10

Because I seek God, and I am his, I will not want for anything good physically, financially, emotionally, and in every other area of my life.

Additional Scriptures:
Jeremiah 29:11; Psalm 132: 15; Psalm 23:1; Deuteronomy 11:14; Philippians 4:6; Joel 2:26

Action Tips:
- ➢ Be faithful in paying your tithes and offerings.
- ➢ Provoke God's blessings through your giving. As you give to the work of God, give to other people too. –I Kings 17:8-16.
- ➢ Thank God in faith for his supernatural provision, and expect it.

~~34~~
SCRIPTURE WORKS FOR RENEWAL OF YOUTH

Those that be planted in the house of the LORD shall flourish in the courts of our God. They shall still bring forth fruit in old age; they shall be fat and flourishing; -Psalm 92:13-14

It is God's will that we enjoy a good old age; one lived in joy, prosperity, strength, and sound health. We can enjoy a life free of pain. We can also enjoy renewal of our youth. He has promised to satisfy us with long life. We will live long, enjoy our old age, and be satisfied. His will is not for us to be sick or in ill health. He has also promised we will bear fruit in old age, meaning we will be relevant even in our old age! Thank you, Jesus!

He did it in the lives of Abraham, Moses, Joshua, Caleb and many others in the bible. He will do it in your life too, if you desire it and ask him for it. You can advance in age and still have your mind alert, your eyes not dimmed, and your strength intact. Make his word your daily vitamins. Take it daily and believe him to renew your strength.

Anchor Scriptures:

But they that wait upon the LORD shall renew their strength; they shall mount up with wings as eagles; they shall run, and not be weary; and they shall walk, and not faint. —Isaiah 40:31

Who satisfieth thy mouth with good things; so that thy youth is renewed like the eagle's. - Psalms 103:5

He fills my life with good things, so that I stay young and strong like an eagle. - Psalms 103:5 (GNT)

Moses was 120 years old when he died, yet his eyesight was clear, and he was as strong as ever. -Deuteronomy 34:7 (NLT)

I am still as strong today as I was in the day that Moses sent me; my strength now is as my strength was then, for war and for going and coming. Joshua 14:11 (ESV)

They will still yield fruit in old age; they shall be full of sap and very green, -Psalm 92:14

Prayer:

I thank you Lord because you are satisfying my mouth with good things, and blessing me with good health. My youth is renewed like the eagles. My strength too is renewed. I shall run, and not be weary; I shall walk, and not faint. You fill my life with good things and I stay young and strong. I am strong and not weak. As my days so shall my strength be. As you were with Moses and his eyes were not dim nor his strength diminished at the age of 120 years, I also receive the same grace, in the name of Jesus. Because you are no respecter of persons, I declare that my eyes shall not be dim.

As Caleb testified that his strength in old age was same as in the days of his youth, I too receive the same blessing and grace, in the name of Jesus. My strength will not diminish with each passing year. I declare that I eat right, exercise right, and my life is filled with the goodness of God. My mind is alert, I enjoy divine health in my old age, and a closer walk with God. I am a blessing to my generation and even generations unborn, and I bear fruit in old age. In Jesus' name I have prayed.

Declaration of Faith:

❖ *If they obey and serve him, they shall spend their days in prosperity, and their years in pleasures.* —Job 36:11

In the name of Jesus, I spend my days in prosperity and my years are pleasurable to the glory of God.

> ❖ *Thy shoes shall be iron and brass; and as thy days, so shall thy strength be. —Deuteronomy 33:25*

The older I get, the stronger I become, according to the word of God. So indeed shall it be, in Jesus' name.

> ❖ *He said, "If you listen carefully to the LORD your God and do what is right in his eyes, if you pay attention to his commands and keep all his decrees, I will not bring on you any of the diseases I brought on the Egyptians, for I am the LORD, who heals you." - Exodus 15:26 (NIV)*

I receive the grace to continually listen to, and obey the Lord my God. I will pay attention to his commands and do what is right in his sight. Therefore, I will not experience any sickness and diseases associated with aging, in Jesus' name. Every weakness disappears from my body. I am strong and able all the days of my life, even to my old age.

Additional Scriptures:
Isaiah 46:4; Deuteronomy 7:15; 3 John 2; Psalms 71:9

~~35~~
SCRIPTURE WORKS FOR RESTORATION

And I will restore to you the years that the locust hath eaten, the cankerworm, and the caterpiller, and the palmerworm, my great army which I sent among you. Joel 2:25

You know that old saying "don't cry over spilled milk"? Well, as children of God we have every reason not to. Why? Our God restores! He will restore your health; he will restore your finances; he will restore your home; he will restore your peace; he will restore your career...Whatever the enemy has stolen from you, our God can, and will, restore it. Not only that, he will restore it seven folds (Proverbs 6:31)! Hallelujah! See why we should celebrate instead? Don't be caught discouraged, or looking dejected. Believe his word and rejoice in anticipation of God's restoration; because HE WILL RESTORE!

Anchor Scriptures:
But if he is found, he shall restore sevenfold; he shall give up all the goods of his house. Proverbs 6:31

When the LORD turned again the captivity of Zion, we were like them that dream. Psalm 126:1

I know that, whatsoever God doeth, it shall be for ever: nothing can be put to it, nor any thing taken from it: and God doeth it, that men should fear before him. Ecclesiastes 3:14

Prayer:
Faithful God, I thank you. You are a God that cannot lie. I agree with your word today, and by faith, I receive restoration of everything the enemy has stolen from my life. My health, finances, family, freedom, home, job...are all restored, in the name of Jesus. Your word says when the thief is caught, he shall restore back seven fold. Every thief in my life is caught today, in the name of Jesus; and I receive seven fold restorations of all I have lost in my life, in Jesus mighty name. My captivity is turned around, and your glory fills my life, so I am like them that dream. I seal all my blessings and miracles with the blood of Jesus, for whatsoever you do, Lord is forever. Thank you Lord!

Declaration of Faith:
> ❖ *And I will restore to you the years that the locust hath eaten, the cankerworm, and the caterpiller, and the palmerworm, my great army which I sent among you. -Joel 2:25*

I receive restoration of all the wasted years of my life. Everything I have lost in the past due to disobedience, are now restored back to me because I am reconciled to my Lord, in Jesus' name.

> ❖ *Thou hast enlarged my steps under me, that my feet did not slip. -Psalm 18:36*

In the name of Jesus, God is enlarging my steps and bringing me into his original plan and purpose for my life. He is catapulting me to greatness; and placing me where I am supposed to be in his divine plan.

Additional Scriptures:
Job 42:10; 2 Chronicles 7:14; Jeremiah 30:17; Isaiah 61:7

~~36~~
SCRIPTURE WORKS FOR REVELATION

For there is nothing hid, which shall not be manifested; neither was any thing kept secret, but that it should come abroad. -Mark 4: 22

I use this scripture so often, from finding little items like missing wallets or car keys, for example, to solving more complex problems both physical and spiritual...and it works each time (just like all of God's word)! If you're confused about anything; need the truth about a situation exposed; or if you need revelation on an issue, then tap into this scripture by faith. Don't forget all of God's word works, and we can believe them just as we find them in the bible.

Anchor Scriptures:

"I will instruct thee and teach thee in the way which thou shalt go: I will guide thee with mine eye" Psalm 32:8

The sheep listen to [the Shepherd's] voice and heed it, and he calls his own sheep by name and brings (leads) them out. -John 10:3

But when He, the Spirit of Truth (the Truth-giving Spirit) comes, He will guide you into all the Truth (the whole, full Truth). For He will not speak His own message [on His own authority]; but He will tell whatever He hears [from the Father; He will give the message that has been given to Him], and He will announce and declare to you the things that are to come [that will happen in the future]. -John 16:13 (AMP)

The entrance of thy words giveth light; it giveth understanding unto the simple. -Psalms 119:130

That the LORD thy God may shew us the way wherein we may walk, and the thing that we may do. -Jeremiah 42:3

Prayer:
Father, I thank you that there is nothing hid, which shall not be manifested; and every secret will be brought to light. Therefore, I pray that you will reveal the truth about this situation (specify situation). I pray that every secret act will be exposed and your name will be glorified. In Jesus' name I pray you teach me what to do, and what actions to take.

Help me to listen for your voice and to recognize it. Lead me out of all confusion I'm in. I receive clarity in my spirit and mind today. I have clear directions from you, Lord, and I take the right steps. I receive light from your word and have an understanding of the current issues and the solution. Thank you Lord for the revelation knowledge I receive from you today.

Declaration of Faith:
❖ *He revealeth the deep and secret things: he knoweth what is in the darkness, and the light dwelleth with him. –Daniel 2:22*

I receive revelation from you today, Lord. Everything in the dark that is causing confusion in my life is being brought to the light in Jesus' name.

❖ *But God hath revealed them unto us by his Spirit: for the Spirit searcheth all things, yea, the deep things of God. -1 Corinthians 2:10*

Holy Spirit, Revealer of deep and secret things, search and reveal all to me regarding this situation (specify situation) in Jesus' name.

Additional Scriptures:
John 8:32; Jeremiah 33:3; Mark 9:23; Job 12:22

~~37~~
SCRIPTURE WORKS FOR SALVATION

"Jesus saith unto him, I am the way, the truth, and the life: no man cometh unto the Father, but by me." John 14:6

There is only one way to God – Jesus Christ. He is the way, the truth, and the life. It is only through him that we can spend eternity in heaven. It is important that we are saved through the blood of Jesus. It is also important that we see as many as we know saved. In addition to sharing the message of salvation with them, we can also pray them into the kingdom of God! The word of God says "No man can come to me, except the Father which hath sent me draw him: and I will raise him up at the last day." -John 6:44. Let us pray that the Lord draws the unsaved, and break off every hindrance to their salvation.

Anchor Scriptures:
"Neither is there salvation in any other: for there is none other name under heaven given among men, whereby we must be saved." Acts 4:12

"And everyone who calls on the name of the Lord will be saved." Acts 2:21 (NIV)

The eyes of your understanding being enlightened; that ye may know what is the hope of his calling, and what the riches of the glory of his inheritance in the saints - Eph 1:18

Prayer:
Father your word says no one comes unto you unless you

draw him. Therefore, I ask today that you draw (person's name) unto you, in the name of Jesus. I thank you because you have assured us that no one who comes to you will be rejected. In the name of Jesus, (person's name) will come to you, and will have a divine encounter with you. I pray that every hold of Satan and religion over their lives is broken and destroyed, in the name of Jesus. They detest sin, and begin to thirst and yearn after righteousness. The eyes of their understanding will be enlightened, and they will understand what the hope of your calling is. I believe your word, and I know that you are more than able. I thank you today because it is done, in the name of Jesus.

Declaration of Faith:
> ❖ *And it shall come to pass, that whosoever shall call on the name of the Lord shall be saved. - Acts 2:21*
>
> *No man can come to me, except the Father who has sent me draw him: and I will raise him up at the last day. -John 6:44*
>
> *Blessed are they which do hunger and thirst after righteousness: for they shall be filled. —Matthew 5:6*

In the name of Jesus I pray that (person's name) will be drawn unto you, by the power of the Holy Spirit. I pray that they begin to thirst and yearn after righteousness and that they begin to call upon the name of the Lord for their own salvation.

Additional Scriptures:
John 3:16; Colossians 1:14; John 1:12; Romans 6:23

~~38~~
SCRIPTURE WORKS FOR SPIRITUAL GROWTH

But seek first his kingdom and his righteousness, and all these things will be given to you as well. -Matthew 6:33 (NIV)

There is absolutely nothing wrong in praying and desiring the blessings of God on our lives. In fact, it is actually in line with God's will for us. He wants to bless us way more than we can ever think or imagine (Ephesians 3:20). However, we must set our priorities right. Seeking things, outside of a relationship with God, is futile. It may look like it works at first, but it won't last. It will be void of the peace and stability that we find only in God.

When we make seeking and pleasing God our priority, he blesses us with, not just things, but his peace, joy, stability, sound health and mind, favor, honor, protection…blessings money can never buy. So let's get it right today, and continually seek him with a sincere heart because we love him; not because we want something from him. He has promised we will find him when we seek him with all our hearts (Jeremiah 29:13).

Anchor Scriptures:

Like newborn babies, you must crave pure spiritual milk so that you will grow into a full experience of salvation. Cry out for this nourishment, -1 Peter 2:2 (NLT)

…As the hart panteth after the water brooks, so panteth my soul after thee, O God. –Psalm 42:1

Let this mind be in you, which was also in Christ Jesus: -Philippians 2:5

For who hath known the mind of the Lord, that he may instruct him? But we have the mind of Christ. -1 Corinthians 2:16

For this cause we also, since the day we heard it, do not cease to pray for you, and to desire that ye might be filled with the knowledge of his will in all wisdom and spiritual understanding; - Colossians 1:9

But grow in grace, and in the knowledge of our Lord and Saviour Jesus Christ. To him be glory now and forever. Amen. -2 Peter 3:18

But the fruit of the Spirit is love, joy, peace, longsuffering, gentleness, goodness, faith,
Meekness, temperance: against such there is no law. –Galatians 5:22-23

Prayer:
Father, in the name of Jesus, I receive a renewed thirst for you, your ways and your word. I will continually crave fellowship with you Lord, and will advance to full maturity in Christ. I pray today that my spirit man will not be malnourished. My soul will always pant after you, O Lord. In the name of Jesus, I know, and have, the mind of Christ. As I seek you Lord, I find you. I pray that you fill me with the knowledge of your will in all wisdom and spiritual understanding. In the name of Jesus, I grow in grace, and in the knowledge of our Lord and Savior, Jesus Christ. I declare that the fruit of the Spirit is manifesting in my life from today. I have love, joy, peace, longsuffering, gentleness, goodness, faith, meekness and self control. My eyes will continue to be enlightened through the word of God, and I will never be a cast-away, in Jesus' name.

Declaration of Faith:
❖ *But seek ye first the kingdom of God, and his righteousness; and all these things shall be added unto you.* -Matthew 6:33

In the name of Jesus, my desire will be to always seek you first and not things.

I pray that the God of our Lord Jesus Christ, the Father of glory, may give unto me the spirit of wisdom and revelation in the knowledge of him: -Based on Ephesians 1:17

Additional Scriptures:
Philippians 1:6; Colossians 2:6-7; Matthew 5:48

Action Tips:
- Begin your days with God. Get up earlier than usual and spend time in fellowship with God every day. Make out the time; even if you start with 10 minutes each morning, it is something.
- Stick to the time you have decided to separate for the Lord; and consistently keep your appointment with God. He will reward your faithfulness and before long, you will find yourself spending more time with him.
- Read the word daily. Expect him to speak to you, and he will.
- Obey God always. Give his word preeminence in your life.
- Listen to anointed messages.
- Detach from distractions and anything that you know hinders your spiritual growth.
- Pray without ceasing, in the Spirit and in your understanding. As you thirst for God, he will visit you and you will grow in him.

~~39~~
SCRIPTURE WORKS FOR THANKSGIVING & PRAISE

Give thanks in all circumstances, for this is God's will for you in Christ Jesus. -1 Thessalonians 5:18 (NIV)

Thanksgiving and praise triggers miracles. Thanksgiving and praise will move God to deliver you like he did for Paul and Silas in the prison (Acts 16:25-26); It will usher you into a realm of unexplainable favor; it will fight your battles while you hold your peace; and give you victory, making you a winner in life. If you have done all, and nothing seem to be working switch to Praise and Thanksgiving! If all is working as you desire, don't forget to lift up your voice in praise of God, because that will seal your testimony.

Anchor Scriptures:
I will praise thee, O LORD, with my whole heart; I will shew forth all thy marvellous works. -Psalm 8:1

As they began to sing and praise, the LORD set ambushes against the men of Ammon and Moab and Mount Seir who were invading Judah, and they were defeated. -2 Chronicles 20:22 (NIV)

Yours, LORD, is the greatness and the power and the glory and the majesty and the splendor, for everything in heaven and earth is yours. Yours, LORD, is the kingdom; you are exalted as head over all. -1 Chronicles 29:11(NIV)

Therefore I will give thanks unto thee, O LORD, among the

heathen, and I will sing praises unto thy name. -2 Samuel 22:50

Let them praise his name in the dance: let them sing praises unto him with the timbrel and harp. -Psalm 149:3

But thanks be to God, which giveth us the victory through our Lord Jesus Christ. -1 Corinthians 15:57

Prayer:
To you, O Lord, be all glory, honor, praise and majesty. You are the Most High God, the Almighty, the Everlasting King, the Eternal Rock of Ages; the Omnipotent, Omnipresent God. I lift my hands this day and just want to bless your holy name. Yours, Lord, is the greatness and the power; and the glory; and the majesty; and the splendor; for everything in heaven and earth is yours. Yours, Lord, is the kingdom; you are exalted as head over all. I praise your name in the dance and with my songs. I thank you for all you have done for me in the past, what you are doing in the present and what you have planned for my future. Blessed be your name, my Lord and Master. In Jesus' name I have praised.

Declaration of Faith:
Therefore I will give thanks unto thee, O LORD, among the heathen, and I will sing praises unto thy name. 2 Samuel 22:50

Blessed be the Lord, who daily loadeth us with benefits, even the God of our salvation. Selah. He that is our God is the God of salvation; and unto GOD the Lord belong the escape from death. Psalm 68:19-20

Additional Scriptures:
Ephesians 5:19-20; Psalm 100:4; Psalm 9:1; Psalm 95:2; 1 Corinthians 15:57

~~40~~
SCRIPTURE WORKS FOR TITHES & OFFERINGS

Honour the Lord with thy substance, and with the firstfruits of all thine increase: so shall thy barns be filled with plenty, and thy presses shall burst out with new wine. Proverbs 3:9-10

I love to say we tithe, so things will not be tight. That is just my little reminder to myself, of the benefits of tithing. When we tithe, the devourer is rebuked for our sakes and he cannot steal our blessings. When we tithe, what we get in return goes beyond money, to what money cannot buy, like protection and peace, for example. Tithing opens us up to God's blessings in all areas of our lives. It shows our obedience to God, and that we trust him. It is also a form of worship. If you do not tithe, I urge you to get started. The benefits are beyond the scope of this book. But know that when you give God his 10 percent, he not only make the rest enough, but opens you up to unimaginable favor and blessings.

Anchor Scriptures:
Bring ye all the tithes into the storehouse, that there may be meat in mine house, and prove me now herewith, saith the Lord of hosts, if I will not open you the windows of heaven, and pour you out a blessing, that there shall not be room enough to receive it. And I will rebuke the devourer for your sakes, and he shall not destroy the fruits of your ground; neither shall your vine cast her fruit before the time in the field, saith the Lord of hosts. And all nations shall call you blessed: for ye shall be a delightsome land, saith the Lord of hosts. -Malachi 3:10-12

Prayer:
Father, I thank you for all the provisions you have given me. I thank you even for the ability to earn income. I am grateful for your love and for constantly meeting my needs.

Today, I bring all my tithes, as you have commanded me, in joy and gratitude. I thank you because every devourer is rebuked for my sake, and they will not destroy the fruits of my ground. I thank you that my vine shall not cast her fruit before the time in the field; and all nations are calling me blessed as the windows of heaven are opened for me. Blessings are being poured on me, and there is not enough room to receive it. As I am blessed, I become a channel of blessing to others too, in Jesus' name.

Declaration of Faith:
> ❖ *Give, and it shall be given unto you; good measure, pressed down, and shaken together, and running over, shall men give into your bosom. For with the same measure that ye mete withal it shall be measured to you again. -Luke 6:38*

I receive a bountiful harvest as I give to the work of God. I receive the favor of God in great measure. People are giving unto me, according to God's word, in Jesus' name. I have favor with God and with man.

> ❖ *Honor the Lord with your wealth and with the firstfruits of all your produce; then your barns will be filled with plenty, and your vats will be bursting with wine. –Proverbs 3:9-10(NIV)*

Lord, as I honor you with my tithes and offering, I receive honor in return and I declare that I have plenty and will never lack. I receive surplus, in Jesus' name.

Additional Scriptures:
2 Corinthians 9:7; Deuteronomy 26:13-15; Exodus 25:2; Proverbs 11:24

Action Tips:
> ➢ Give cheerfully, always.
> ➢ Give in faith.
> ➢ Pray over your tithe and offering personally, giving God thanks and honor.

~~41~~
SCRIPTURE WORKS FOR VICTORY

For the LORD your God is the one who goes with you to fight for you against your enemies to give you victory." -Deuteronomy 20:4 (NIV)

We win when we hand over our battles to the Lord; trusting that we are protected and shielded in his love. God will never lose a battle. The bible describe him as "Mighty in battle" (Psalm 24:8), and we read several accounts of him triumphantly leading his people in battle and conquering for them. Sometimes they don't even need to fight physically (Exodus 14:13; 2 Chronicles 20:22), yet they win! What he instructs you to do may look strange, embarrassing or foolish to the human mind (like the Israelites marching round Jericho in Joshua 6), but if we will trust and obey him, we will always emerge victorious.

Anchor Scriptures:
Giving thanks unto the Father, who has made us fit to be partakers of the inheritance of the saints in light: Who hath delivered us from the power of darkness, and hath translated us into the kingdom of his dear Son: -Colossians 1:12-13

What do ye imagine against the LORD? he will make an utter end: affliction shall not rise up the second time. -Nahum 1:9

I have pursued mine enemies, and overtaken them: neither did I turn again till they were consumed. I have wounded them that they were not able to rise: they are fallen under my feet. - Psalms 18:37-38

The LORD is my rock, my fortress and my deliverer; my God is my rock, in whom I take refuge. He is my shield and the horn of my salvation, my stronghold. -Psalms 18:2 (NIV)

Prayer:
Father, in the name of Jesus, I thank you that you are my Rock, my Fortress, my Deliverer, my Shield and the Horn of my Salvation. I know that in you I have victory every day of my life, when I entrust my battles to you. Lord I invite you into every war, seen or unseen that is coming against me. I ask that you take over. You are the Lord, strong and mighty in battle, the unconquerable Conqueror. You are the mighty Warrior, who never retreats in battle. Lord, I decree today that I have pursued my enemies, and overtaken them: neither did I turn again till they were consumed. I have wounded them that they were not able to rise: they are fallen under my feet, in the name of Jesus. I live a life of victory in all things, and at all times. The Lord has made an end of every one of my struggles and afflictions. In Jesus' name, afflictions shall not arise a second time in my life. The victories the Lord has given me are permanent, in the name of Jesus. I am delivered out of the power of darkness, and translated into the kingdom of God's dear Son, Jesus Christ. I thank you, Jesus, for making me partake of eternal victories in life.

Declaration of Faith:
❖ *Blessed be the LORD my strength, which teacheth my hands to war, and my fingers to fight: -Psalm 144:1*
In the name of Jesus I receive wisdom, and the power to do spiritual warfare, and conquer. I declare that I fight every battle by the power and anointing of the Holy Spirit, and I am victorious.

❖ *Ye shall not fear them: for the LORD your God he shall fight for you. -Deuteronomy 3:22*
Lord, I hand this battle over unto you. I hold my peace

and watch you fight for me, in Jesus' name.

Additional Scriptures:
Matthew 21:44; Ephesians 6:12, 14; Zechariah 4:6

~~42~~
SCRIPTURE WORKS FOR WARFARE & BREAKING CURSES

For we wrestle not against flesh and blood, but against principalities, against powers, against the rulers of the darkness of this world, against spiritual wickedness in high places. -Ephesians 6:12

And they overcame him by the blood of the Lamb, and by the word of their testimony; and they loved not their lives unto the death. – Revelation 12:11

Whether we admit it or not, there is always some spiritual warfare going on in every life. From battling to live a righteous life before God, to waging war against the devil so you can reach your destiny. The good news is we will win every time, when we have God by our side! He has given us power in the blood of Jesus; the name of Jesus; the word of God; and the Holy Spirit. We are to *"… take unto you the whole armour of God, that ye may be able to withstand in the evil day, and having done all, to stand."* -Ephesians 6:13

Anchor Scriptures:
(For the weapons of our warfare are not carnal, but mighty through God to the pulling down of strong holds;) Casting down imaginations, and every high thing that exalteth itself against the knowledge of God, and bringing into captivity every thought to the obedience of Christ; -2 Corinthians 10:4-5

Behold, they shall surely gather together, but not by me: whosoever shall gather together against thee shall fall for thy sake. - Isaiah 54:15

Christ hath redeemed us from the curse of the law, being made a curse for us: for it is written, Cursed is every one that hangeth on a tree: - Galatians 3:13

Surely there is no enchantment against Jacob, neither is there any divination against Israel: according to this time it shall be said of Jacob and of Israel, What hath God wrought! -Numbers 23:23

And to Jesus the mediator of the new covenant, and to the blood of sprinkling, that speaketh better things than that of Abel. -Hebrews 12:24

And the LORD said unto Satan, The LORD rebuke thee, O Satan; even the LORD that hath chosen Jerusalem rebuke thee: is not this a brand plucked out of the fire? -Zechariah 3:2

Saying, Touch not mine anointed, and do my prophets no harm. - 1 Chronicles 16:22

Stand fast therefore in the liberty wherewith Christ hath made us free, and be not entangled again with the yoke of bondage. -Galatians 5:1

The soul that sinneth, it shall die. The son shall not bear the iniquity of the father, neither shall the father bear the iniquity of the son: the righteousness of the righteous shall be upon him, and the wickedness of the wicked shall be upon him. -Ezekiel 18:20

He that committeth sin is of the devil; for the devil sinneth from the beginning. For this purpose the Son of God was manifested, that he might destroy the works of the devil. -1 John 3:8

If the Son therefore shall make you free, ye shall be free indeed. -John 8:36

Whoso diggeth a pit shall fall therein: and he that rolleth a stone, it will return upon him. -Proverbs 26:27

Prayer:
In the name of Jesus, I take cover under the blood of Jesus. I come against every plan and strategy of the evil one. I declare today that no evil attack shall prosper over my life. I cast down every evil imagination against my life. I destroy every habitation of evil in my life. Your word says surely they shall gather, but because their gathering is not of you, it shall not stand. In the name of Jesus Christ, I command every evil gang up and meetings against me to begin to fall. Every one gathering to do me harm shall fall for my sake in the name of Jesus. Everyone digging a pit for me shall fall into their own pit. Every stone rolled against me shall return upon him that rolls it in agreement with the word of the Lord, in the name of Jesus.

I break every curse against my life, because Christ has redeemed me from the curse of the law. There is no enchantment against (your name), no divination against me that shall prosper in the name of Jesus. The blood of Jesus that speaks better things than the blood of Abel speaks on my behalf today. I come against every evil force by the blood of Jesus. Satan, the Lord rebuke you over my life, in the name of Jesus, because I am his chosen one. I am a "touch-not" entity because I am his anointed, and his word commands you to touch not his anointed and do his prophets no harm. Because I am under a new covenant by the blood of Jesus, I break every generation curse and covenants over my life, in the name of Jesus. I receive my total freedom and liberty and work in the freedom wherewith Christ has made me free. I will never again be entangled with the yoke of bondage, in Jesus mighty name.

Declaration of Faith:
And the Lord shall deliver me from every evil work, and will preserve me unto his heavenly kingdom: to whom be glory for ever and ever. Amen. -2 Timothy 4:18

But he answered and said, Every plant, which my heavenly Father hath not planted, shall be rooted up. -Matthew 15:13

In the name of Jesus, I command every plantation of evil to be rooted up from my life. Everything that is not of God, I command you OUT of me in the name of Jesus. Holy Spirit of God, I invite you into my spirit, soul and body. Take your place in my life, in Jesus' name.

No weapon that is formed against me shall prosper; and every tongue that shall rise against me in judgment I condemn now. This is the heritage of the servants of the LORD, and their righteousness is of me, saith the LORD. -Based on Isaiah 54:17

❖ *Christ hath redeemed us from the curse of the law, being made a curse for us: for it is written, Cursed is every one that hangeth on a tree: -Galatians 3:13*

I have been redeemed from every curse, and will never be under bondage again, in Jesus' name!

Additional Scriptures:
Genesis 12:3; Ephesians 6:13; Proverbs 26:2; James 4:7; Job 5:21

Action Tips:
➢ Don't be in strife.
➢ Walk in love. Love is the strongest weapon of all! Without love, prayers are hindered. Your prayers shall not be hindered in Jesus' name.
➢ Remember we wrestle against the devil, not people.

~~43~~
SCRIPTURE WORKS FOR WISDOM

If any of you lack wisdom, let him ask of God, that giveth to all men liberally, and upbraideth not; and it shall be given him. But let him ask in faith, nothing wavering. For he that wavereth is like a wave of the sea driven with the wind and tossed. -James 1:5-6

You can never go wrong when you operate in the wisdom of God. It will save you unnecessary trauma and headaches. Operating in God's wisdom will also bring you honor; and make even your opposition respect and submit to you. Some years back, I had an agreement with someone who later came back, abruptly changing the arrangement. It was obvious they were ready for battle, but I felt the Holy Spirit leading me to be quiet, and not debate it with them. So, I kept my peace, and the conversation ended there. I however went on my knees and pleaded my case with God using Proverbs 21:1 *"The king's heart is in the hand of the Lord, as the rivers of water: he turneth it whithersoever he will."* asking that God would turn their hearts in my favor. I rested my case, believed my prayers were answered, and went about my business as usual. Few weeks later, I got a call back from them in a very different tone of voice, "suggesting" we go an alternate route, which perfectly matched what I had requested of the Lord! God's wisdom will bring you on top each time, and save you from costly reactions and mistakes.

Anchor Scriptures:
If you don't know what you're doing, pray to the Father. He loves to help. You'll get his help, and won't be condescended to when you ask for

it.

Ask boldly, believingly, without a second thought. People who "worry their prayers" are like wind–whipped waves. -James 1:5-6 (MSG)

That your faith should not stand in the wisdom of men, but in the power of God. -1 Corinthians 2:5

The mouth of the righteous speaketh wisdom, and his tongue talketh of judgment. -Psalms 37:30

And they were not able to resist the wisdom and the spirit by which he spake. -Acts 6:10

Prayer:
Father, in the name of Jesus, I pray for your wisdom in my life today, particularly in this situation (mention situation). I ask that you guide me on what to do, and the right steps to take. Fill my heart with your wisdom, and when I open my mouth to speak, let the wisdom of God be released out of my mouth. My words shall build others, not break them, in the name of Jesus. Holy Spirit, I invite you to take permanent residence in my life, and lead me in all my dealings. I approach your throne boldly, and I ask in faith, nothing wavering. My faith shall not be in the wisdom of men, but in the power of God. My mouth and tongue shall speak wisdom at all times.

I am able to help others out of their predicament through the wisdom of God that is dwelling in me. I will be a solution bearer after the order of Joseph and Daniel, in the name of Jesus. I am wise, intelligent, diligent and faithful. I use the gift of wisdom in me to advance the kingdom of God, and glorify God's name. None shall be able to resist the wisdom of God in me, but will rather recognize that the Spirit of God dwells in me, and give glory to God.

Declaration of Faith:
❖ *And the spirit of the Lord shall rest upon him, the spirit of*

> *wisdom and understanding, the spirit of counsel and might, the spirit of knowledge and of the fear of the Lord; -Isaiah 11:2*

In the name of Jesus, the Spirit of the Lord rests upon me. The Spirit of wisdom and understanding, the Spirit of counsel and might is in me. I have the Spirit of knowledge, and of the fear of the Lord.

> ❖ *For I will give you words and wisdom that none of your adversaries will be able to resist or contradict. -Luke 21:15 (NIV)*

I receive words and wisdom from you Lord, that none of my adversaries and opponents shall be able to resist or contradict, in the name of Jesus. As I speak, they shall all be in awe of you, giving glory to God.

> *But the wisdom that is from above is first pure, then peaceable, gentle, and easy to be entreated, full of mercy and good fruits, without partiality, and without hypocrisy. -James 3:17*

Lord, I receive this kind of wisdom from you that is pure, peaceable, gentle, and easy to be entreated, full of mercy and good fruits; without partiality and without hypocrisy, in Jesus' name.

Additional Scriptures:
Proverbs 1:7; Ecclesiastes 7:12; Psalm 111:10

Action Tips:
- Ask the Lord for wisdom, and you will receive if asked in faith.
- Seek the Lord regarding every situation, and be guided before you take any action.
- Practice listening for his voice. It can come through his word, other people, as a still small voice etc. But anyway it comes, wait for a confirmation. It must also be in line with the word of God.
- Keep wise companions.

~~44~~
SCRIPTURE WORKS FOR WIVES
(Praying God's Word over Your Husband)

For what knowest thou, O wife, whether thou shalt save thy husband? or how knowest thou, O man, whether thou shalt save thy wife? -1 Corinthians 7:16

Marriage was, and still is, God's idea from the beginning. Wives are created to be helpers to their husbands. One vital and powerful way to accomplish this is by praying for your husband. Below are suggested prayers/confessions from the word of God that women can pray for their husbands. Husbands can also pray these over themselves too.

Anchor Scriptures:
That the God of our Lord Jesus Christ, the Father of glory, may give unto you the spirit of wisdom and revelation in the knowledge of him: The eyes of your understanding being enlightened; that ye may know what is the hope of his calling, and what the riches of the glory of his inheritance in the saints -Ephesians 1:17-18

That he would grant you, according to the riches of his glory, to be strengthened with might by his Spirit in the inner man; -Ephesians 3:16

For this cause we also, since the day we heard it, do not cease to pray for you, and to desire that ye might be filled with the knowledge of his will in all wisdom and spiritual understanding; That ye might walk worthy of the Lord unto all pleasing, being fruitful in every good work, and increasing in the knowledge of God; Strengthened with all might, according to his glorious power, unto all patience and longsuffering with joyfulness; -Colossians 1:9-11

And the LORD God said, It is not good that the man should be alone; I will make him an help meet for him. -Genesis 2:18

Casting down imaginations, and every high thing that exalteth itself against the knowledge of God, and bringing into captivity every thought to the obedience of Christ; -2 Corinthians 10:5

Finally, brethren, whatsoever things are true, whatsoever things are honest, whatsoever things are just, whatsoever things are pure, whatsoever things are lovely, whatsoever things are of good report; if there be any virtue, and if there be any praise, think on these things. -Philippians 4:8

And you shall love the LORD your God with all your heart, and with all your soul, and with all your might. -Deuteronomy 6:5

Prayer:

Father, in the name of Jesus, I thank you for my husband, (insert his name). Thank you for bringing us together as one. Thank you for your grace over his life and for guiding and protecting him always. I pray in the name of Jesus that according to your word, you will give him wisdom and revelation in the knowledge of you. I pray my husband's eyes of understanding be enlightened, and that he will know and fulfill the calling of God in his life. My husband (insert name) lives a purposeful and Holy Spirit guided life, in the name of Jesus.

My husband is filled with the knowledge of God's will. He has wisdom and spiritual understanding and walks worthy of the Lord unto all pleasing. He is faithful in every good work and increases continually in the knowledge of God. He enjoys strength from the Lord, and is patient, long suffering, and full of joy. He is an excellent father, after the order of our Heavenly Father; and a faithful husband. He loves me, his wife, as Christ loves the church. The peace of God guards his heart, and he has guidance and direction in all his endeavors. By the help of the Holy Spirit, my husband casts down every imagination that is contrary to the will of God and brings his thoughts captive under the obedience of Christ. He thinks only of things that are true, honest, just, pure, lovely, virtuous, praise-worthy, and of good report. He loves and serves the Lord his God with all his heart, soul and might; and he meditates constantly on the word of God. His ways are prosperous and he enjoys good success in life. His companions are wise men who love the Lord, and he is steadfast in his obedience to the Lord, our God. In Jesus' name I pray.

Declaration of Faith:
> ❖ *Wives, submit yourselves unto your own husbands, as unto the Lord. -Ephesians 5:22*

In Jesus' name, I submit to my husband as unto the Lord. I honor and respect him at all times.

> ❖ *Her husband is respected at the city gate, where he takes his seat among the elders of the land. —Proverbs 31:23*

Father, I ask that you bestow honor on my husband. He will be respected by all that comes in contact with him. I pray that you fill him with wisdom that commands respect and give honor to your name, in Jesus' name.

Additional Scriptures:
1 Corinthians 11:3, 9; Proverbs 14:1; Ephesians 5:24, 25

Action Tips:
- Cover your husband in prayers all the time.
- Respect and honor your husband.
- Be submissive to your husband.
- Encourage an atmosphere of love, and joy in your home.

~~45~~
SCRIPTURE WORKS - DAILY FAITH DECLARATIONS

For the word of God is quick, and powerful, and sharper than any twoedged sword, piercing even to the dividing asunder of soul and spirit, and of the joints and marrow, and is a discerner of the thoughts and intents of the heart. -Hebrews 4:12

Anchor Scriptures

Psalm 105:15; Romans 8:11; Isaiah 22:22; Psalm 118:17; Isaiah 25:8; John 14:19; 1 Corinthians 15:55; Exodus 23:26; Romans 8:1; 2 Timothy 1:7; 1 Corinthians 2:16

- ❖ Every force of wickedness ganging up against me shall fall for my sake, in Jesus' name.
- ❖ It shall be well with me, my destiny, and my finances.
- ❖ I shall be above only and never beneath.
- ❖ I and my children are for signs and wonders.
- ❖ I receive, by the anointing of the Holy Spirit, an end to all satanic attacks, in Jesus' name.
- ❖ I receive an end to confusion and indecision in my life.
- ❖ No demon, principalities or powers, wickedness in high places or satanic agents shall be able to touch me because I am anointed of the Lord.
- ❖ I command everything good that is dead in my life to come alive now, by the resurrection power that raised Jesus from the dead.
- ❖ I speak to every organ, bone, tissues, my brain:

come alive in the name of Jesus!
- My future is secured in Jesus Christ.
- Every door of favor shut against me, I command you to open in the name of Jesus.
- I shall not die but live to declare the works of the Lord in the land of the living.
- Because death is swallowed up in victory, no one in my family shall die young.
- The number of my days, I shall fulfill; in the name of Jesus!
- The power of death is broken over my life.
- Because Jesus lives I shall live also.
- Today, every depression in my life ends, in the name of Jesus.
- God makes every area of my life perfect. He comforts me on every side.
- God changes my story today. He is mighty in my life always.
- I take cover under the blood of Jesus. No arrow of the evil ones targeted against me shall touch me.
- No weapon formed against me shall prosper.
- I am blessed going out, and blessed coming in.
- Everything I lay my hands on prospers.
- Thank You Lord because my sins are remembered no more!
- Father, I receive and enjoy your mercy on my life today; and I thank you for forgiving me.
- I am free from any and every condemnation, in Jesus' name.
- I understand the love of God for me.
- I am his dearly beloved and walk after the law of the Spirit of God, and not of the flesh!
- The works of my hands are blessed.
- God has not given me the spirit of fear, so I fear not!
- The Lord has given me a sound mind; and I have

the mind of Christ.
- ❖ Every work of darkness around me is destroyed in Jesus' name.
- ❖ I am blessed with all spiritual blessings in heavenly places.
- ❖ Every door of goodness shut against me are now opened, in the name of Jesus.
- ❖ The favor of God locates me today.
- ❖ I will not be found among the failures again, in the name of Jesus.
- ❖ I will not be counted among the poor.
- ❖ I radiate the glory of God and all men are calling me blessed.

SALVATION PRAYER

If we confess our sins, he is faithful and just to forgive us our sins, and to cleanse us from all unrighteousness. 1 John 1:9

Neither is there salvation in any other: for there is none other name under heaven given among men, whereby we must be saved. —Acts 4:12

For whosoever shall call upon the name of the Lord shall be saved. Romans 10:13

Prayer:

Heavenly Father, I come to you this day, confessing my sins. I believe in the death and resurrection of Jesus Christ; I thank you for the provision you have made for me to be saved through the blood of your son, Jesus. I believe your word that says whosoever shall call upon the name of the Lord shall be saved. Lord Jesus, I call on you to save and reconcile me back to God. I renounce my sins, and I confess that I believe that Jesus Christ is the Son of God. Right now, I accept Jesus as my Lord and Savior.

Lord Jesus, come into my life, and live your life through me. Fill me with your Holy Spirit and give me the grace to live for you all the days of my life. I thank you Lord for saving me. In Jesus' name I pray. Amen.

Printed in Great Britain
by Amazon